Leading Business Teams

Leading Business Teams

How Teams Can Use Technology and Group Process Tools to Enhance Performance

Robert Johansen
Alexia Martin
Robert Mittman
Paul Saffo

Institute for the Future

David Sibbet
Suzyn Benson

Graphic Guides

 ADDISON-WESLEY PUBLISHING COMPANY
Reading, Massachusetts • Menlo Park, California • New York
Don Mills, Ontario • Wokingham, England • Amsterdam • Bonn
Sydney • Singapore • Tokyo • Madrid • San Juan • Milan • Paris

Library of Congress Cataloging-in-Publication Data

Leading business teams: how teams can use technology and group
  process tools to enhance performance / Robert Johansen . . . [et. al.].
    p.   cm.
  Includes bibliographical references.
  ISBN 0-201-52829-0
  1. Work groups. 2. Work groups—Data processing.   I. Johansen,
Robert.
HD66.L43   1991
658.4'036'0285—dc20   90-45598
                                                              CIP

This book is in the Addison-Wesley Series on Organization Development.
Editors: Edgar H. Schein, Richard Beckhard

ISBN 0–201–52829–0
  2 3 4 5 6 7 8 9 10 BA 9594939291

To the participants in the Groupware Users' Project, for their many ideas and pioneering spirit.

Other Titles in the Organization Development Series

Parallel Learning Structures: Increasing Innovation in Bureaucracies
Gervase R. Bushe and A.B. Shani

1991 (52427)

Parallel learning structures are technostructural interventions that promote system-wide change in bureaucracies while retaining the advantages of bureaucratic design. This text serves as a resource of models and theories built around five cases of parallel learning structures that can help those who create and maintain them be more effective and successful. For those new to parallel learning structures, the text provides practical advice as to when and how to use them.

The Strategic Management Process: Integrating the OD Perspective
David Hitchin and Walter Ross

1991 (52429)

Written for CEOs, general managers, OD professionals, and strategic-planning specialists, this text integrates the OD perspective into the strategic-management process. This approach begins with the authors' belief that building and sustaining a healthy, high-performance organization is dependent upon the fact that people are the key to organizational success, and that their management is critical to successful strategic planning and execution. The authors' philosophy and suggestions for the strategic management of both profit and nonprofit organizations are presented.

Managing in the New Team Environment: Skills, Tools, and Methods
Larry Hirschhorn

1991 (52503)

This text is designed to help manage the tensions and complexities that arise for managers seeking to guide employees in a team environment. Based on an interactive video course developed at IBM, the text takes managers step by step through the process of building a team and authorizing it to act while they learn to step back and delegate. Specific issues addressed are how to give a team structure, how to facilitate its basic processes, and how to acknowledge differences in relationships among team members and between the manager and individual team members.

The Conflict-Positive Organization: Stimulate Diversity and Create Unity
Dean Tjosvold

1991 (51485)

This book describes how managers and employees can use conflict to find common ground, solve problems, and strengthen morale and relationships. By showing how well-managed conflict invigorates and empowers teams and organizations, the text demonstrates how conflict is vital for a company's continuous improvement and increased competitive advantage.

Change by Design
Robert R. Blake, Jane Srygley Mouton, and Anne Adams McCanse

1989 (50748)

This book develops a systematic approach to organization development and provides readers with rich illustrations of coherent planned change. The book involves testing, examining, revising, and strengthening conceptual foundations in order to create sharper corporate focus and increased predictability of successful organization development.

Organization Development in Health Care
R. Wayne Boss

1989 (18364)

This is the first book to discuss the intricacies of the health care industry. The book explains the impact of OD in creating healthy and viable organizations in the health care sector. Through unique and innovative techniques, hospitals are able to reduce nursing turnover, thereby resolving the nursing shortage problem. The text also addresses how OD can improve such bottom-line variables as cash flow and net profits.

Self-Designing Organizations: Learning How to Create High Performance
Susan Albers Mohrman and Thomas G. Cummings

1989 (14603)

This book looks beyond traditional approaches to organizational transition, offering a strategy for developing organizations that enables them to learn not only how to adjust to the dynamic environment in which they exist, but also how to achieve a higher level of performance. This strategy assumes that change is a learning process: the goal is continually refined as organizational members learn how to function more effectively and respond to dynamic conditions in their environment.

Power and Organization Development: Mobilizing Power to Implement Change
Larry E. Greiner and Virginia E. Schein

1988 (12185)

This book forges an important collaborative approach between two opposing and often contradictory approaches to management: OD practitioners who espouse a "more humane" workplace without understanding the political realities of getting things done, and practicing managers who feel comfortable with power but overlook the role of human potential in contributing to positive results.

Designing Organizations for High Performance
David P. Hanna

1988 (12693)

This book is the first to give insight into the actual processes you can use to translate organizational concepts into bottom-line improvements. Hanna's "how-to" approach shows not only the successful methods of intervention, but also the plans behind them and the corresponding results.

Process Consultation, Volume 1: Its Role in Organization Development, Second Edition
Edgar H. Schein

1988 (06736)

How can a situation be influenced in the workplace without the direct use of power or formal authority? This book presents the core theoretical foundations and basic prescriptions for effective management.

Organizational Transitions: Managing Complex Change, Second Edition
Richard Beckhard and Reuben T. Harris

1987 (10887)

This book discusses the choices involved in developing a management system appropriate to the "transition state." It also discusses commitment to change, organizational culture, and increasing and maintaining productivity, creativity, and innovation.

Organization Development: A Normative View
W. Warner Burke

1987 (10697)

This book concisely describes and defines the theories and practices of organization development and also looks at organization development as change in an organization's culture. It is a useful guide to the field of organization development and is invaluable to managers, executives, practitioners, and anyone desiring an excellent overview of this multifaceted field.

Team Building: Issues and Alternatives, Second Edition
William G. Dyer

1987 (18037)

Through the use of the techniques and procedures described in this book, managers and consultants can effectively prepare, apply, and follow up on the human processes affecting the productive functioning of teams.

The Technology Connection: Strategy and Change in the Information Age
Marc S. Gerstein
1987 (12188)
This is a book that guides managers and consultants through crucial decisions about the use of technology for increasing effectiveness and competitive advantage. It provides a useful way to think about the relationship between information technology, business strategy, and the process of change in organizations.

Stream Analysis: A Powerful Way to Diagnose and Manage Organizational Change
Jerry I. Porras
1987 (05693)
Drawing on a conceptual framework that helps the reader to better understand organizations, this book shows how to diagnose failings in organizational functioning and how to plan a comprehensive set of actions needed to change the organization into a more effective system.

Process Consultation, Volume II: Lessons for Managers and Consultants
Edgar H. Schein
1987 (06744)
This book shows the viability of the process consultation model for working with human systems. Like Schein's first volume on process consultation, the second volume focuses on the moment-to-moment behavior of the manager or consultant rather than on the design of the OD program.

Managing Conflict: Interpersonal Dialogue and Third-Party Roles, Second Edition
Richard E. Walton
1987 (08859)
This book shows how to implement a dialogue approach to conflict management. It presents a framework for diagnosing recurring conflicts and suggests several basic options for controlling or resolving them.

Pay and Organization Development
Edward E. Lawler
1981 (03990)
This book examines the important role that reward systems play in organization development efforts. By combining examples and specific recommendations with conceptual material, it organizes the various topics and puts them into a total systems perspective. Specific pay approaches such as gainsharing, skill-based pay, and flexible benefits are discussed and their impact on productivity and the quality of work life is analyzed.

Work Redesign
J. Richard Hackman and Greg R. Oldham

1980 (02779)

This book is a comprehensive, clearly written study of work design as a strategy for personal and organizational change. Linking theory and practical technologies, it develops traditional and alternative approaches to work design that can benefit both individuals and organizations.

Organizational Dynamics: Diagnosis and Intervention
John P. Kotter

1978 (03890)

This book offers managers and OD specialists a powerful method of diagnosing organizational problems and of deciding when, where, and how to use (or not use) the diverse and growing number of organizational improvement tools that are available today. Comprehensive and fully integrated, the book includes many different concepts, research findings, and competing philosophies and provides specific examples of how to use the information to improve organizational functioning.

Career Dynamics: Matching Individual and Organizational Needs
Edgar H. Schein

1978 (06834)

This book studies the complexities of career development from both an individual and an organizational perspective. Changing needs throughout the adult life cycle, interaction of work and family, and integration of individual and organizational goals through human resource planning and development are all thoroughly explored.

Matrix
Stanley M. Davis and Paul Lawrence

1977 (01115)

This book defines and describes the matrix organization, a significant departure from the traditional "one man-one boss" management system. The author notes that the tension between the need for independence (fostering innovation) and order (fostering efficiency) drives organizations to consider a matrix system. Among the issues addressed are reasons for using a matrix, methods for establishing one, the impact of the system on individuals, its hazards, and what types of organizations can use a matrix system.

Feedback and Organization Development: Using Data-Based Methods
David A. Nadler

1977 (05006)

This book addresses the use of data as a tool for organizational change. It attempts to bring together some of what is known from experience and research and to translate that knowledge into useful insights for those who are thinking about using data-based methods in organizations. The broad approach of the text is to treat a whole range of questions and issues considering the various uses of data as an organizational change tool.

Designing Complex Organizations
Jay Galbraith

1973 (02559)

This book attempts to present an analytical framework of the design of organizations, particularly of types of organizations that apply lateral decision processes or matrix forms. These forms have become pervasive in all types of organizations, yet there is little systematic public knowledge about them. This book helps fill this gap.

Organization Development: Strategies and Models
Richard Beckhard

1969 (00448)

This book is written for managers, specialists, and students of management who are concerned with the planning of organization development programs to resolve the dilemmas brought about by a rapidly changing environment. Practiced teams of interdependent people must spend real time improving their methods of working, decision making, and communicating, and a planned, managed change is the first step toward effecting and maintaining these improvements.

Organization Development: Its Nature, Origins, and Prospects
Warren G. Bennis

1969 (00523)

This primer on OD is written with an eye toward the people in organizations who are interested in learning more about this educational strategy as well as for those practitioners and students of OD who may want a basic statement both to learn from and to argue with. The author treats the subject with a minimum of academic jargon and a maximum of concrete examples drawn from his own and others' experience.

Developing Organizations: Diagnosis and Action
Paul R. Lawrence and Jay W. Lorsch

1969 (04204)

This book is a personal statement of the authors' evolving experience, through research and consulting, in the work of developing organizations. The text presents the authors' overview of organization development, then proceeds to examine issues at each of three critical interfaces: the organization-environment interface, the group-group interface, and the individual-organization interface, including brief examples of work on each. The text concludes by pulling the themes together in a set of conclusions about organizational development issues as they present themselves to practicing managers.

About the Team of Authors

Robert Johansen, Senior Research Fellow and Director, New Technologies Program at Institute for the Future (IFTF), has worked for nearly 20 years in the fields of telecommunications and computing. He has focused on the business, social, and organizational effects of new systems. Working with vendors, he has examined the potential of specific new product concepts and assisted in the development of marketing plans. Working with users, he has assisted them in understanding their information needs and opportunities, in making judgments about which media are most appropriate for them to use, and in tracking the effects of new information systems. A social scientist with an interdisciplinary background, he holds a BS degree from the University of Illinois, and a Ph.D. from Northwestern University.

David Sibbet, President, Graphic Guides, is an organizational consultant and graphic designer who, for almost 20 years, has been helping people work together by opening their ability to communicate in groups and within larger organizational structures. His explorations in interactive, graphic communication, structured experiences for adult development, and collaborative process design are helping define a new genre of consulting. He received a B.S. in physics and English from Occidental College and an M.S. in journalism from Northwestern University.

Suzyn Benson is a senior writer, editor, and designer with over 15 years' experience. She was a vice president at Graphic Guides and a core team member on the Groupware Users' Project during the writing of this book. She is now working independently on various projects from her base in San Francisco. Suzyn has a diverse background in writing, publishing, and working with a wide range of media. She has also worked with projects in instructional design and photography.

Alexia Martin, Research Fellow, IFTF, combines expertise in systems analysis and organization development. In the systems area, she has planned, designed, and implemented large-scale management information and end-user systems in a variety of industries. Further, Alexia conducts market research and market planning related to customer needs for service, support, and training. Alexia is currently conducting research on organizational restructuring to meet current and future needs and expectations of the workforce. She received her B.A. degree in political science from San Francisco State University and her M.S. in organization development from the University of San Francisco.

Robert Mittman, Research Fellow and Director, Teleservices Program at IFTF, has worked extensively in information systems and telecommunications policy. His areas of activity include forecasting the business and policy environment, projecting the impact of new technologies, and evaluating market opportunities for information and communications companies. He has developed forecast models of the U.S. markets for teleconferencing products and electronic information services. He has worked with communications suppliers to identify potentially lucrative value-added information services. Robert holds a B.S. in electrical engineering, an M.S. in computer science, and an M.P.P. in public policy analysis, all from the University of California at Berkeley.

Paul Saffo is a Research Fellow at IFTF, specializing in the long-term commercial and policy impacts of new information technologies. Paul is also a Contributing Editor for *Infoworld* Magazine, a columnist for *The Los Angeles Times,* and he is a member of the Editorial Board of the Journal of Computers and Society. Paul holds a B.A. from Harvard College, an LL.B. from Cambridge University, and a J.D. from Stanford Law School.

Foreword

The Addison-Wesley Series on Organization Development originated in the late 1960s when a number of us recognized that the rapidly growing field of "OD" was not well understood or well defined. We also recognized that there was no one OD philosophy, and hence one could not at that time write a textbook on the theory and practice of OD, but one could make clear what various practitioners were doing under that label. So the original six books launched what has since become a continuing enterprise, the essence of which was to allow different authors to speak for themselves instead of trying to summarize under one umbrella what was obviously a rapidly growing and highly diverse field.

By the early 1980s the series included nineteen titles. OD was growing by leaps and bounds, and it was expanding into all kinds of organizational areas and technologies of intervention. By this time, many textbooks existed as well that tried to capture the core concepts of the field, but we felt that diversity and innovation were still the more salient aspects of OD.

Now as we move into the 1990s our series includes twenty-seven titles, and we are beginning to see some real convergence in the underlying assumptions of OD. As we observe how different professionals working in different kinds of organizations and occupational communities make their case, we see we are still far from having a single "theory" of organization development. Yet, a set of common assumptions is surfacing. We are beginning to see patterns in what works and what does not work, and we are becoming more articulate about these patterns. We are also seeing the field connecting to broader themes in the organizational sciences, and new theories and theories of practice are being presented in such areas as conflict resolution, group dynamics, and the process of change in relationship to culture. The new titles in the series address current themes directly: Johansen et al.'s *Leading Business Teams,* for example, draws the link between OD skills and emerging electronic tools for teams; Tjosvold's *The Conflict-Positive Organization,* connects to a whole research tradition on the dynamics of collaboration, competition, and conflict; Hirschhorn's *Managing in the New Team Environment* contains important links to psychoanalytic group theory; Bushe and Shani's *Parallel Learning Structures* presents a seminal theory of large-scale organization change based on the institution of parallel systems as change agents; and Hitchin and Ross's *The Strategic Management Process* looks at the connection between strategic planning theory and practice and implementation through OD interventions.

As editors we have not dictated these connections, nor have we asked authors to work on higher-order concepts and theories. It is just happening, and it is a welcome turn of events. Perhaps it is an indication that OD may be reaching a period of consolidation and integration. We hope that we can contribute to this trend with future volumes.

Cambridge, Massachusetts   Richard H. Beckhard
New York, New York   Edgar H. Schein

Preface

In this book we explore the intersection of technology and business teams, a new and largely uncharted area that goes by several labels, including the one we use: *groupware*—a term that encompasses both electronic and nonelectronic tools for teams. In the pages that follow, we chart the groupware terrain, explore various groupware building blocks, offer a perspective on how to turn groups into teams, and describe several examples of groupware applied to actual business practice.

In *Part I* we begin with the essential motivation for groupware: pain. The driving force behind the sudden interest in groupware is the acute need to enhance team effectiveness in order to enhance overall *business competitiveness*. Groupware is less about a technology in search of a problem than it is about problems in search of useful tools. Because maps are crucial to any exploration, this chapter provides several, both conceptual and literal.

In *Part II* we describe the basic building blocks available for turning groupware ideas into business realities, and we cover promising electronic groupware tools and systems. The primary focus is on infrastructure—existing electronic systems like voice and electronic mail that can be put to use as groupware. In general, we have concluded that you are better off adding a little groupware to existing infrastructure than adding a lot of groupware where you have to create a new infrastructure. Not all groupware is large and complex, and in this section we explore a few low-tech examples, including copyboards and Total Quality groupware. In addition, we speculate about what future groupware infrastructures could offer when they eventually arrive.

Technology matters in the groupware success equation, but team dynamics matter much more. The most important aspects of groupware focus on the *group* more than the *ware*. *In Part III*, therefore, we focus on the human side of the groupware equation. Some of the chapters in this section explore the role of facilitators, describe surprises lurking in group dynamics, offer pointers on how to tell if a team is in trouble, and provide lessons from the real world. Other chapters explore what happens when groups form by accident, and caution against the risk of overselling the team concept.

In *Part IV* we present a composite profile of groupware in action, assembled from our experiences in the field with a variety of business teams. The identities of companies and individuals involved in our research for this book have been concealed, but the lessons—including some surprises—are clear.

In *Part V* we set forth two additional reports from the field. The first describes use of groupware in a cross-cultural context, and the second covers the use of groupware in educational environments. Both provide important insights useful to business users trying to make sense of groupware in their own organizations.

In *Part VI*, the final section, we present our vision of future directions for teams and tools. The bottom line is that groupware as a concept is here to stay, whether the word "groupware" survives or not. In the epilogue, we present our vision of the approaches that will offer the biggest long-term payoffs and what steps organizations can take *now* to move toward this long-term success.

This book is written in small chunks, rather than long chapters. We have done this intentionally in a handbook style so that team members can draw on specific sections for specific needs. It can be read like a magazine, rather than a traditional linear text. One of our findings is that business team members have little time, so we have written this book in brief packets of information geared toward the needs of business team leaders and team members.

Acknowledgments

This is a book about teams, written by a team. For all of us involved, it has been our most stimulating and satisfying team experience ever.

Our team grew out of work David Sibbet and I were doing with major corporations. David has worked for over 20 years pioneering the development of graphic language and process thinking for business management. His background in public affairs education and leadership training at Coro Foundation, as well as years of experience in organizational consulting for private corporations, has led him to study organizations from a very practical standpoint. How does one get people to cooperate about overall direction? How can management groups lead in today's business environment?

My perspective comes from 20 years of studying emerging information technologies, with a special emphasis on user points of view. "Groupware" (defined early on as computer and telecommunications tools to help teams collaborate more effectively) was one emerging technology area my colleagues and I at the Institute for the Future (IFTF) had identified and begun to study.* In my

---

*Our book called *Groupware: Computer Support for Business Teams* (New York: The Free Press, 1988) mapped the groupware field as an emerging technology.

work with Sibbet, it became clear that what he was doing with groups using graphic frameworks and processes was also a form of "groupware," although it certainly was not electronic. Some teams even jokingly referred to him as a "bionic Macintosh."

If what David does is groupware, what about other non-electronic group processes that are important to the performance of a team? What is the relationship between the electronic and nonelectronic forms of groupware? How can organizations take advantage of both electronic and nonelectronic forms of groupware while avoiding whatever pitfalls might arise from this effort? It was questions like these that led to creation of the Groupware Users' Project. Sibbet and I, in several lengthy airplane conversations and later with our colleagues and clients, came up with the idea of a project geared toward companies that are trying to increase the performance of their work teams. The idea was to work with a small group of noncompeting organizations drawn from different industry sectors and perspectives. We would work with each company, first to assist them in improving the performance of one or a small number of selected teams, and second to generalize from this experience and create a practical groupware guidebook geared toward business team leaders. We would also encourage exchanges among the various user organizations pursuing groupware. The project is a joint venture of Institute for the Future (IFTF) and Graphic Guides, Inc., David Sibbet's organization. *Leading Business Teams* is the result of the first year's research and activities from this ongoing project.

Identifying companies to participate in the project was very interesting. We spoke with about 50 major companies, keeping in mind our desire to enlist noncompeting companies with different industry perspectives. Interest in groupware and teams was very high—higher than we expected. What was hard was finding companies who had the right types of teams ready to work with us at the right time. Business teams often do not know what their needs are, especially with regard to the possible use of new technology or processes. There is a lesson here regarding the world of business teams: Teams move very fast, and it is hard to get their attention. Once you are on board with them, the pace is frenetic. This project looked to the future of business teams, while most teams are intensely committed to the present—with few incentives to look up from immediate concerns. We had to play by their rules in order to get the opportunity to look beyond immediate pressures.

Six companies participated in the first year of the Groupware Users' Project. Each contributed a different set of organizational issues and different types of teams. Meanwhile, at both IFTF and Graphic Guides, we had parallel experiences with other teams that were directly relevant to our experiences with this project. The Groupware Users' Project grew in ways that were a bit different than we expected, but the first year certainly resulted in many real-world experiences regarding business teams and the tools they might use.

We are drawing from this experience base as we write. Our target reader is a leader of business teams, someone who has a strong interest in making his or her team perform well. It is too early for a rigid "how to" book (actually, such a book may never be possible in the dynamic world of business teams), but it is possible to present pointers that have been learned from experience to date. We also have thought about other audiences, beyond team leaders, as we have written this book—organizational development and training professionals, emerging technology planners in users' organizations, prospective vendors, and service providers, for example.

Our goal is not to present an academic report. Rather, we offer a practical—though certainly tentative—guide, assembled from field research results and anecdotes. At first, we envisioned this book as a "Strunk and White" for team leaders (Strunk and White's *Elements of Style* is a reference text consulted frequently by writers and editors). Later, we settled on a "magazine" model for the book, and it was this perspective that drove our efforts down the home stretch.

Most major reports or books I have worked on feel like glaciers by the time they reach the latter stages of completion. There is little excitement left among the authors; it is very difficult to steer or even make small changes in direction; and the piece just keeps crunching along toward closure. The magazine model allowed us to divide this book into smaller chunks that we could continue revising as the overall book evolved. As with magazines, a variety of contributors fed material to "editors," who also did some writing. Although the magazine idea was attractive in terms of its flexibility and vigor, we realized that this material also had to fit together into a larger whole.

Suzyn Benson and Paul Saffo were the central "editors" for this book. They provided a guiding vision, building on what our team was learning in the field; both contributed key articles. Alexia

Martin and Robert Mittman were vital core team members, each working with individual companies in the field, analyzing results, and working with the rest of the team to figure out what the results really meant. Both contributed major writing efforts to this book.

Several people in the companies we worked with became part of our core team, and their ideas added greatly to the results. At our team meetings throughout the year, we had progress reports on how the overall vision was evolving. We also had many discussions and debates about what this overall vision should be.

David Sibbet worked with most of the client companies at some point. David was our link to nonelectronic groupware: He was our conscience regarding group process theory and models of the universe. David also put forth his talents to illustrate the chapters in this book.

Marshall Clark, cartoonist extraordinaire, deserves special thanks for contributing his humorous and insightful cartoons, all of which were done spontaneously as he sat in the back of the University of Arizona's decision support room in Tucson during our year-end client meeting. Tomi Nagai-Rothe and Andrea Saveri both contributed specific sections to the book, providing useful outside experiences for our core project team. Tomi Nagai-Rothe, Thom Sibbet, and Suzanne Masica all contributed greatly during the editorial and production stages, which proved to be a considerable challenge to all our creativity and endurance. Judy Buchan heroically translated that effort into this final book.

Menlo Park, California   R.J.

Contents

Part I
Understanding Team Needs

1

The Need for Groupware

Pain!

"You'd better hurry and publish your findings," a consultant friend from Tokyo said recently. "I just saw a complete spread on groupware in one of our computer magazines. That usually means it's less than a year before we've devoured everything about a new topic."

The article, like many appearing in current journals, dealt with the odd-lot collection of electronic software programs that

"Good morning! If you have a few minutes I'd like to show you something that I think could solve your problem. . . ."

aim at improving group performance and productivity in business teams. Some are well known, like electronic mail (E-mail) programs that are especially user friendly; some allow more exotic applications, like screen sharing at a distance; and others are new database filters and integrators that turn networks into powerful tools for competitive advantage.

On the hardware front, infrastructure developments, expanded storage capacity, laptops, lasers, scanners, and multimedia systems present a broiling environment still aglow with promise. And behind the news are R&D projects in firms all over the western world trying to bring the fragmenting PC phenomenon to rein with solutions that foster collaboration, information integration, and team support. So what is this notion of groupware and why is it important?

Groupware as Conceptual Anchor

Groupware on one level is a conceptual anchor. People make sense of fast-breaking business developments by giving them names. Some stick; some don't; but they serve the purpose of rallying attention at crucial stages in development. In the high seas of the current business climate, anchors are important. The groupware "anchor" reminds us that the main focus is the business team and the tools it needs to get its job done.

Groupware as a Set of Tools

Groupware on another level is a collection of electronic tools. It's clear that business teams are here to stay, and they need tools to help get their jobs done. Tools that expressly support teams are groupware. Within the next decade, managers will expect all their systems—from computers to telephones—to provide real support for their collaborative work as well as their individual work.

Groupware as a Banner for Action

Groupware on a third level is a banner for a group of innovative businesses that aren't waiting for the field to define itself. Large installed bases of equipment and mounting costs demand return on investment. The innovations of these companies are in many cases actually pushing the software manufacturers and other vendors. It's their needs that drive the real market for groupware today.

It was a small group of these "definers" that made the Groupware Users' Project possible. "Users," in this case, refers not to passive consumers but to active creators. The participants were large organizations responding to a set of real pains. They were on a mission to find out which groupware tools really worked to get them going, and if they couldn't find any, to create them.

Businesses interested in groupware are not just indulging in a fad. Groupware is too complex and challenging to attract the impatient. The environmental and social conditions under which business teams and their leaders are operating make progress not only difficult but at times downright painful. "We are in pain," is the simple message we hear from team leaders. A quick look at the list below showing current forces on business teams and their leaders tells why.

"Pains" Creating the Need for Groupware

Pace

Fast and getting faster. Some say cycle times for product development and distribution will be the key competitive differentiator in the 1990s. *And* if you don't have quality and price, you aren't even in the game.

Competition

Fierce and going global.

Alliances

Messy and essential in high-tech and growing in all sectors. And the people you need are never in the same place.

Central Information Systems versus Line Business Areas

Decentralized autonomy over systems was fun for a while, until the lack of integration became too expensive. The move is on to connect, but the move toward decentralization still continues in many parts of the business. Indeed, information technologies are allowing the possibility of simultaneous centralization and decentralization.

Electronic Marketplace

Finally practical, with fueling factors such as interexchange standards and pocket computers growing, but it is still a tricky process for most businesses.

Teams and Flexible Organizations

The "big wave" industry leaders will have to catch. Still confusing to functionally organized corporations that grew up in clearly defined markets.

If these are the forces driving the fascination with groupware, as reflected by the first year of the Groupware Users' Project, then the underlying, compelling need can be expressed simply as the need for team effectiveness. And team effectiveness involves the basics, such as

- understanding visions and mandates,
- gathering the right participants,
- communicating with team members,
- evaluating information,
- making timely decisions,
- communicating about progress to the larger organization,
- completing projects on schedule, and
- tracking and learning from customer reactions.

But clearly the basics aren't what they used to be. The forces of change are hitting businesses faster and faster. Competition can reduce the advantage of a new product introduction to a matter of months. A change in a tariff can wipe out the profit margins for an entire product line overnight. Business teams frequently have members constantly out of the office, and are often made up of individuals based at two or more locations, sometimes in different countries. Like the business environment they are in, business teams are changing constantly.

In spite of the difficulties, teams increasingly are seen by many as the basic organizational building block of the future, especially for innovative companies. Decisions need to be made as fast as the business environment is changing, and organizations are learning that decisions are made most effectively when the structure for making them is spread among smaller decision-making units (that is, teams) that are close to the market and the customer, rather than centralized with a few decision makers at the top.

Is Groupware Always Electronic?

Right now "groupware" refers primarily to electronic tools, but participants in the Groupware Users' Project have been unanimous in indicating that the work processes and designs the tools reinforce — or disrupt — are more fundamental than the tools themselves.

Electronic groupware often provides powerful tools to users with neither blueprints to follow nor training to help them. A project management program won't help any manager finish a project on schedule if he or she doesn't understand the dynamics of managing people. Nor will page layout and group editing programs produce high-quality documents unless someone on the team understands the editorial development process and the fundamentals of graphic design.

Team Collaboration

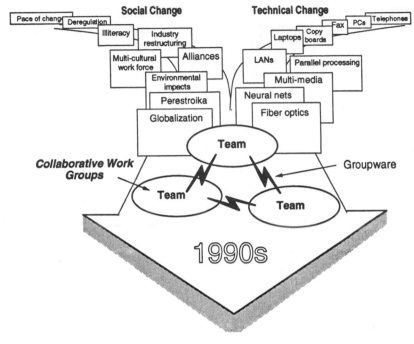

Forces Driving Groupware

Such dilemmas brought the Groupware Users' Project to look beyond electronics to the conceptual tools used by organizational development consultants and process-oriented managers to get results from teams. It turns out that many of these tools—like style typologies, process models, meeting-facilitation systems—are structured like software and are simply intended for human "operating systems" directly. These tools often are essential to choosing and implementing electronic groupware.

Is groupware always electronic? No. If electronic tools were groupware's first words, then nonelectronic methodologies and techniques are emerging as its sentences and paragraphs. The stories and poetry are yet to come.

What Is Nonelectronic Groupware, Anyway?

Gandhi said, "The means are just the ends in process." If you care about where you are going to end up, you'd better think about how you are getting there. When you don't, curious problems emerge, and well-intentioned but inappropriate choices can make things worse.

For example, fax machines can add a welcome visual dimension to the immediacy of telephone conversations. Still, fax alone is insufficient when executives want to see the face behind the voice at the other end, thus making video teleconferencing attractive. But some issues, like building trust, are so fundamental that nothing less than a face-to-face meeting will do. In that case, what the group may need is a good off-site meeting that focuses on team building.

In another case, a team might not have the means to get together face-to-face and a videoconference may be essential to get a sense of who the other person really is. To look at all these variables with any perspective, one needs the conceptual tools growing out of the organizational behavior and development fields.

Process consultants help teams understand *how* they can reach their goals. They frequently will create a model to focus a team on project goals, as well as to create a shared reference so the team can understand and talk about how its members are working together. During the life of a project, being able to discuss problems—as well as successes—is critical to sustaining high performance. Goals becoming unclear or shifting, new members joining a team or critical members leaving, and budgets or resources changing, are all examples of problems that come up for teams; and having a model that is understood and used by all members facilitates speedy resolution of these and other issues. The process consultant serves the team as a guide along the way.

Groupware could be imagined as a team's mirror—its value is not in the design of the frame or the quality of the glass, but what it reveals about the team. If groupware tools show information as snapshots, that is all the team will see. If the tools mirror the movement of a team and show it as an entire movie, then the team will begin to be able to think about process—how the team works together, its timing, and how it is managed.

With groupware, the ability to think intuitively as well as analytically must play a central part. Successful Japanese executives don't talk a lot; they listen. Successful American executives are expected to talk and interpret. Often they don't listen as well. These differences and others are part of the groupware challenge.

What to Call It?

Computer-supported cooperative work (CSCW)
Workgroup computing
Collaborative computing
Cooperative computing
Interpersonal computing
Coordination technology
Decision conferencing
Computer conferencing
Computer-supported groups (CSG)
Group decision support systems (GDSS)

Computer-assisted communication (CAC)
Augmented knowledge workshops
Interfunctional coordination
Flexible interactive technologies for multiperson tasks
Data interpretation systems (DIS)
Shared systems
Co-technologies
Group support systems (GSS)

As is typical of emerging technologies, naming is a problem. In early stages, the prospectors of a new field try out various names in search of one that can capture the essence of a new idea and communicate it well to people who have never heard of it. Numerous candidate names have appeared for technology supported teams in the past few years, including those listed here. Though each of these names has merit, none is a name to stir the hearts of prospective users.

Peter and Trudy Johnson-Lenz, who work over an electronic information network called EIES (New Jersey Institute of Technology) are credited with first using the term *groupware*. Cal Pava of Harvard is another early user of the word. There were probably other early users of the term, and, as is usual in such cases, it is very difficult to determine who really coined it. The first time we saw the term *groupware* in the mass-market press was in the *Fortune* article called "Software Catches the Team Spirit" (June 1987). Since then the term has come into much wider use, and many network-based products carry the label.

Searching for Groupware Gold

The Japanese computer magazine that carried the feature story on groupware mentioned at the beginning of this chapter also included a whimsical illustration of the promises and pitfalls in the new groupware world. The illustration was of a galleon from the age of exploration. It was navigating the troubled, shark-infested waters of the international business seas, guided by a treasure map. The map charted the ship past the "LAN whirlpools," around the treacherous "Cape of E-mail," and on to an "Isle of Groupware Paradise."

We, of course, don't expect to find an instant paradise after a brief adventure. One thing groupware *isn't* is the next quick fix, or consumable piece of technology to resolve corporate dilemmas. Groupware *can* mirror organizational need and reveal appropriate solutions, both electronic and nonelectronic. But the real groupware "gold" is what individuals bring to their work efforts and what their commitment is to continuous learning and team collaboration.

It's no accident the illustrator chose a metaphor from the age of exploration, with its dangers and hardships. There are many pains for which some form of groupware might provide relief. However, this form of pain relief is years away from a packaged form that can be taken easily. We are still in the exploratory stage, where users take many of the risks and create the forms of groupware that will be most useful to them. In the Groupware Users' Project, we have aimed toward reducing these risks and exploring the early forms of groupware in practical ways. This book reports on those explorations and introduces the maps that we have developed and employed along the way.

2

Mapping the Groupware Territory

The 4-Square Map of Groupware Options and the Team Performance Model

Maps and travel logs were essential equipment for early explorers. Maps served not only to help chart a new course but also to guide the next round of explorers. A well-documented travel log provided credibility, as well as subject matter, for many a good story long after the journey had ended.

Remembering the 4 Ms (Mission, Maps, Memos, and Models), the Group Leader Prepared His Team for Its Task

Simple conceptual maps and frameworks that model organizational behavior are equally important tools for exploring emerging technologies today. New technology means change. And because people resist change, even when it might bring desirable results, organizational researchers have discovered that most people will not change unless they encounter valid data that spell out a need to do so. Carefully chosen research frameworks not only provide data, but they increase its validity.

A second reason underscoring the need for such tools is that the exploration itself needs a focal point for exchange and inquiry. In the information age, language and models are our galleons. A good framework illuminates a subject both by what it embraces and by what it doesn't. Challenges to the frameworks are some of the best clues to new avenues of inquiry.

Say It on a Page

An early goal of the Groupware Users' Project was to create a single-page map that could be placed in front of someone who had never heard about the emerging technology (in this case, groupware) and be used to explain the subject at a general level within five minutes. Within ten minutes, a newcomer should be able to "talk through" the map as he or she asks questions and makes comments about the groupware concept. When frameworks are this clear, then the focus can be on the territory and finding the new patterns within it. The 4-Square Map of Groupware Options satisfied this early need.

We then found that, in fact, we needed two base frameworks. One for taking snapshots—a map that showed all the technology elements and their relationship in some meaningful dimension—and one for showing movies—or the process aspect of the journey. The 4-Square Map of Groupware Options organized the content of our exploration, the tools themselves, and showed how the tools relate to two major aspects of group reality: *time* and *place*. The *Drexler/Sibbet* Team Performance Model™ was brought in and used to talk about group process—that is, to show the movies.

In this chapter we introduce both models in order to help prospective users of groupware make practical sense out of the options. Each prospective user creates, whether consciously or unconsciously, a *pain-frame* that begins from his or her current state of dire need—or *pain*—and looks for ways in which new ideas like groupware might relieve some of the pain. We have found in our early work with groupware users that these two models make this pain-frame process happen faster and more creatively.

A Focus on Functionality: The 4-Square Map of Groupware Options

It makes sense that groupware tools would spring up around the basic configurations that teams must cope with as they work: *time* and *place*.[1] Teams deal with their affairs in the same place at the same time (for example, in meetings), and they must work apart in different places and at different times (for example, with E-mail). They also handle the other two variations—being in different places at the same time (for example, with telephones) and the same place at different times (for example, offices). The groupware options we knew about at the start of the project mapped easily onto this framework (see Fig. 2.1). As with any good framework, it guided us toward new places to look. Here is what we found.

Start with the Most Familiar: Same Time/Same Place

Face-to-face meetings happen at the same time and in the same place. Groupware in this setting is geared toward doing better what people already do: hold meetings. It's the mode in which people feel most comfortable, because most people feel the need to meet face-to-face. At the simple end of the spectrum, *same time / same place,* groupware can be a copyboard (a machine that makes paper copies of whatever is written on a special whiteboard) or a projection system that displays PC screens via a plate that rests atop a standard overhead projector.

This is horseless-carriage groupware, where accepted practices are modified only slightly to include electronic support. At the high-tech end of the spectrum for *same-time / same-place* groupware, consider a room with a workstation for each participant. Figure 2.2 shows an IBM Decision Conference Center in Bethesda, Maryland. IBM in 1990 had 30 similar rooms and had conducted over 2,000 sessions using them.

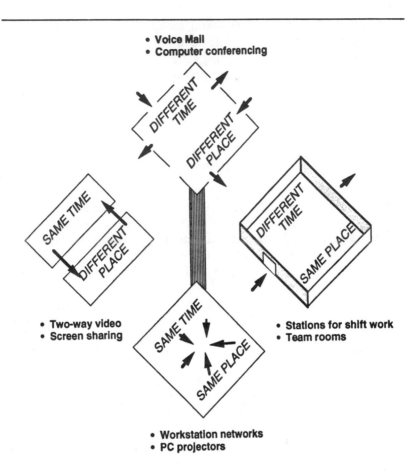

Figure 2.1
4-Square Map of Groupware Options

Special software developed at the University of Arizona helps a group with tasks such as brainstorming, idea organization, stakeholder analysis, ranking, and voting. Participants can type in ideas or vote on items anonymously, simultaneous group writing or analysis can occur, and a written record of the session can be produced at its conclusion. Although researchers have established such "group decision support systems" over the last 20 years, they are now on the verge of being practical for real

Figure 2.2
An IBM "TeamFocus" Room in Bethesda, Maryland.
Photo courtesy of IBM.

business applications. IBM, for example, is now making this system available to customers during an initial exploration of its commercial feasibility.

Meeting without Meetings: Different Time/Different Place

The other extreme from *same time / same place* is *different time / different place*. Here, the focus is on asynchronous communication in a store-and-forward mode, and the need addressed is ongoing coordination. Electronic mail is a common tool in this category, with group-oriented electronic mail usually labeled "computer conferencing" or some such term. Another emerging groupware tool in this area is voice mail.

Whether electronic mail or voice mail, groupware "happens" when a team of users collaborates through the system via software that makes such communication graceful. Each participant checks into the system, sees what has been entered since he or she was last present, makes any comments, and leaves. Beyond simple messages, conversations can be structured around forms that are accepted by the organization or principles about the type of team behavior that should be encouraged (for example, efforts to encourage meeting deadlines).

The key advantage is flexibility—it is often very difficult to assemble team members at the same place, at the same time. The key disadvantages are *different-time/different-place* unfamiliarity (most people are not used to holding meetings that are stretched out over time) and the lack of "real-time" (a curious term) feedback.

If you draw a straight line from *same time/same place* to *different time/different place* on the 4-Square Map, you see the central axis of groupware. Ideally, groupware users want the familiarity of face-to-face with the flexibility of asynchronous media. For the near future, a cautious development strategy is to stay close to the central axis of groupware.

Meetings at a Distance: Same Time/Different Place

On either side of the central axis, however, are two interesting clusters of options. In the short run, the most promising of the two tributary cells is *same time/different place*. This is the notion of an electronic meeting, or teleconference, when participants are geographically separated but are present simultaneously.

Many times it is not possible to get a team together face-to-face. Distance barriers are often too imposing for team members to meet in person, so meetings via electronic means are a practical alternative. Yet the idea here is not to replace travel with telecommunications, as predicted in the 1970s, but to permit more selective use of face-to-face meetings—for example, during critical stages in the life of a team like the kickoff meeting or following the accomplishment of key milestones.

The simplest form of groupware for meetings held at the same time in different places is the conference call (audio teleconference), and it is an important building-block technology. Now that we have entered the era of digital conference call bridges, it is possible to hear all participants clearly and even to interrupt each other without an awkward voice switch (difficult to do during conference calls over many PBXs). It is also possible to exchange PC, fax, or graphic images simultaneously with a conference call. This narrowband teleconferencing is the easiest form of electronic meeting to cost justify, given today's technology.

Beyond the obvious, however, video teleconferencing has also become practical enough that you will not get thrown out of the office by a bean counter (or at least not by most bean counters). The cost of full-motion video codecs (coder/decoders) was halved in the last year, and costs are also dropping for both modular room construction and transmission. The link to personal computing is becoming practical as well, and this link is lowering the cost equation dramatically. Video teleconferencing, finally, is coming of age. And this is the form of *same-time/ different-place* groupware that is often most attractive to prospective users.

Same-time/different-place groupware is likely to be most useful for the goal and role clarification and commitment stages of group process, assuming that orientation and trust building have been done well. Communication at the same time permits immediate feedback, which is important for goal clarification and commitment, because people can see whether their proposals are being accepted and can understand who is signing up to do what. However, it may not be necessary for everyone to be present in the same place. Also, during the implementation of a project, periodic *same-time/different-place* meetings can be useful to provide regular reviews of progress.

Remember the Office: Same Place/Different Time

For some, the final cell in the 4-Square Map of groupware options is the most difficult to imagine: *same place/different time*. But it's a type of tool that's right under our nose—the office. A lot of information is available from a quick walk-through, and the other team members don't have to be present. More specifically, stations for shift work allow teams of people to hand off to other teams to keep a manufacturing line going, for example, or to continue a process of international currency trading around the clock. A bedside workstation in a hospital is another example, where a team of health care providers offers round-the-clock care.

Finally, team rooms provide an example of this form of groupware. As business teams have become more common in the United States, companies have begun providing some teams with special rooms where regular meetings and other ongoing team activities can occur. Team rooms provide a shared "clubhouse" for teams, but they can also be enhanced by various forms of groupware to facilitate group memory, to chart progress toward goals, and otherwise to assist a team in getting its job done. There are shared needs for administrative support, shared filing, and even filtering of information to avoid overload and to identify resources that might be important to the team. Increasingly, we expect to see the emergence of new groupware tools designed for use in team rooms, *same place / different time.*

4-Square Findings

Each of the cells in the 4-Square Map is characterized by focused activity and the development of specific groupware tools. In our review of this work, however, we have been disappointed to learn that people working in each cell tend to be ignorant of groupware options in the other three cells. Such a narrow focus is understandable, given the early stage in the development of this marketplace, but it is also troubling. We suspect that each of the cells represents only a stepping stone toward future capabilities that will cut across the *time / place* matrix.

In trying to gain a perspective for the future of groupware, it is instructive to think back to the early pioneers of groupware—even before it was called that. Doug Engelbart's NLS in the late 1960s and early 1970s, for example, had capabilities within each of the four *time / place* cells. For *same time / same place,* Engelbart had a team room where the moderator had a full workstation and each of the participants had a mouse. Several monitors were recessed within the circle of tables around which everyone sat (see Fig. 2.3). For *different time / different place,* there were shared journals and group writing capabilities; screen sharing, audio links, and even motion video on a split screen were available for *same time / different place.* Finally, *same-place / different-time* capabilities were in place in Engelbart's Augmentation Research Center at Stanford Research Institute so that team members could use the center at any time of the day or night—even if other team members were not present simultaneously.

Today's approaches to groupware, however, are much more focused—with little thought about how distinct capabilities might be orchestrated within the overall activities of a business team. For example, *same-time / same-place* systems emphasize what goes on during meetings. Pre-meeting and post-meeting follow-ups are typically ignored in such systems, even though they are also very important and there are real opportunities for creative products and services.

Figure 2.3
Doug Engelbart and his colleagues at the Augmentation
Research Center, circa 1967 (Stanford Research Institute,
Menlo Park, CA). Photos courtesy of Douglas Engelbart.

Any time/Any place. Stanley M. Davis, in the ground-breaking book *Future Perfect*,[2] has argued convincingly that the concept of *any time / any place* will be standard in the economy of the future. Davis emphasizes shortening to the maximum extent possible the elapsed interval between the customer's identified need and its fulfillment. Similarly, space constraints will be decreased in pursuit of any-place delivery to customers, whenever this is possible. Business teams are taking the lead in creating this economy of the future, and groupware will have to play by the rules of this new game. The rules will require *any-time / any-place* flexibility as soon as possible. Although today's technologies make this a very difficult goal to meet, it is likely to be required by tomorrow's marketplace.

Thus groupware applications can build from the current cells of separation, but the future will be drawn toward fostering *any-time / any-place* operations, with the ability to cut across cells in the current groupware matrix coming into play as needed (see Fig. 2.4).

This is a time to step on to the ridge and take a wider view. Although work down in the valleys of each *time / place* cell is important, premature concentration in any one cell—to the exclusion of the others—is likely to result in blind canyons for either vendors or users of groupware.

Even a view from the ridge of electronic groupware options, however, does not provide enough insight about basic team needs. We found in our work with prospective users that it is necessary to include careful consideration of the team itself, not just the technology. The following model was chosen because it addresses a vital portion of the pain frame that users seek to avoid as they try to make sense out of groupware.

A Focus on Team Process: The Team Performance Model

If it is to be more than a solution looking for a problem, groupware should begin with a compelling user need. In order to understand the needs of business teams, it is necessary to understand the basic ways they work—independent of technology. Where are pains likely to arise in the life of a business team?

Task-oriented teams are trying to get somewhere, produce something, change something, or discover something. Leading such teams requires a focus on direction and movement. So does the problem of implementing groupware. The chorus of advice

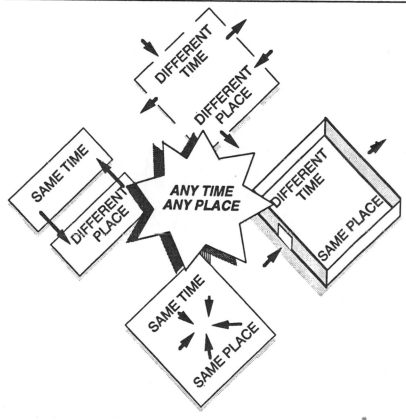

Figure 2.4
4-Square Map of Groupware Options

from advanced software users to neophytes is, "Figure out what
you want to do and how you want to do it *first*—then get the tools."

So we needed a framework to think about team processes
where groupware might have the potential to relieve pain. The
Team Performance Model provides a common sense framework
that we find business people can understand and use easily.
Although there are certainly other models we could have used,
this is the best we have found yet. It not only offers a generic way
to look at the stages of team creation, but it also deals with the
stages involved in sustaining performance. It was developed by

integrating a basic team-building model based on research into group process by Allan Drexler, Marvin Weisbord, and Jack Gibb with the process theories of Arthur M. Young.[3]

Seven Recurring Stages

Group process does not move smoothly. It has stages and deadlines. Developments happen in leaps and plateaus. The life of a business team has times of opportunity and openness, as well as tight spots where constraints are severe. The structure of the Team Performance Model illustrates this interplay between freedom and constraint.

Thus at its simplest, team process can be understood as a movement toward constraint as teams form, and a movement toward freedom as they master constraints. Then the team process moves toward constraint again as new realities enter, and then toward freedom as the new realities are integrated. In real life, the process is as varied as music, but this basic pattern plays throughout. It is represented by the V shape of the model of Fig. 2.5.

If each of these basic directions is divided into parts, one arrives at a seven-stage model describing the generic, recurring stages that teams encounter. Gibb's research suggests the issues of each stage must be addressed in approximate order before people are willing to move on to more complex issues.

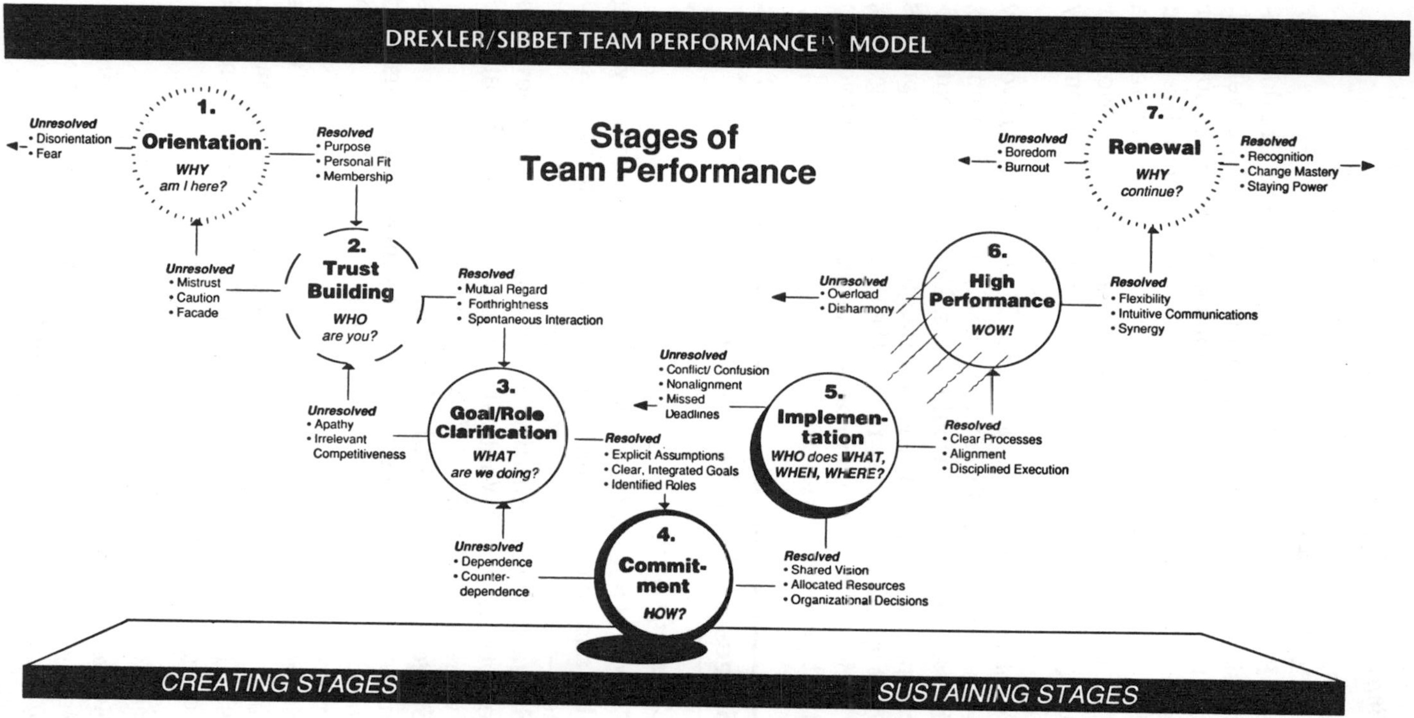
DREXLER/SIBBET TEAM PERFORMANCE™ MODEL
Stages of Team Performance
1. Orientation
WHY am I here?
Unresolved
• Disorientation
• Fear
Resolved
• Purpose
• Personal Fit
• Membership
2. Trust Building
WHO are you?
Unresolved
• Mistrust
• Caution
• Facade
Resolved
• Mutual Regard
• Forthrightness
• Spontaneous Interaction
3. Goal/Role Clarification
WHAT are we doing?
Unresolved
• Apathy
• Irrelevant Competitiveness
Resolved
• Explicit Assumptions
• Clear, Integrated Goals
• Identified Roles
4. Commitment
HOW?
Unresolved
• Dependence
• Counter-dependence
Resolved
• Shared Vision
• Allocated Resources
• Organizational Decisions
5. Implementation
WHO does WHAT, WHEN, WHERE?
Unresolved
• Conflict/ Confusion
• Nonalignment
• Missed Deadlines
Resolved
• Clear Processes
• Alignment
• Disciplined Execution
6. High Performance
WOW!
Unresolved
• Overload
• Disharmony
Resolved
• Flexibility
• Intuitive Communications
• Synergy
7. Renewal
WHY continue?
Unresolved
• Boredom
• Burnout
Resolved
• Recognition
• Change Mastery
• Staying Power
CREATING STAGES
SUSTAINING STAGES

Figure 2.5
Drexler / Sibbet Team Performance™ Model (5.0 Drexler / Sibbet © 1990)

A Project Breakthrough

The Team Performance Model is accompanied the Drexler/Sibbert/Forrester Team Performance Inventory™, a fully developed, normative inventory that queries teams with nine questions for each stage of the model and seven questions about the team leadership.[4] We decided to use the Inventory to generate data about the teams in the project, and as a common framework for aggregating insights and comparing the teams across a company and an industry.

Together the Team Performance Model and the Inventory enabled us to create different team and groupware scenarios, much the way a musician would use a keyboard to create different compositions. Teams move through the stages of process at different speeds, and they repeat the stages in varying ways, moving backward to reclaim understandings that may have been skipped but prove essential.

Stages of Team Performance

Creating Stages

Stage 1: Orientation. As people begin a process anything is possible and the challenge is imagining *why* the team should be formed—what is its purpose and mandate?

Stage 2: Trust Building. Next, people want to know *who* they are working with. "What will you expect of me?" "What level of involvement will I risk?" "Who are you?"

Stage 3: Goal/Role Clarification. The team next turns its attention to *what* it must do. Constraints of language and understanding arise. But without clear goals and roles, the team won't progress very effectively.

Stage 4: Commitment. At some point discussion needs to end and decisions must be made about structure, resources, budgets—all the constraints. The team faces a major turn as it works to agree on *how* to proceed.

Sustaining Stages

Stage 5: Implementation. After commitment, members turn to answering the questions involving *who does what, when, and where.* The timing and sequence of work now must be managed.

Stage 6: High Performance. If methods are mastered, a team will rise above having to think about everything conceptually and can intuitively and flexibly respond to fast-breaking conditions. This results in occasional *WOWs!*

Stage 7: Renewal. High performance isn't a steady state. People get tired. Members change. *"Why continue?"* people wonder. The team must transition to a new process, perhaps at a deeper level of understanding, but nonetheless a new journey.

A feature of the Team Performance Model is that each stage builds on the prior ones in an inclusive way—thus trust and goal clarification become integral to having good implementation and even more important for high performance. The model kept us focused on the fact that process always deals with concrete organizational realities, and that mastering these realities rather than fighting them is a key to the higher-order freedoms of the later stages.

Using the Models in Practice

The model of Fig. 2.6 is a hybrid of the 4-Square Map of Groupware Options and the Team Performance Model. During our

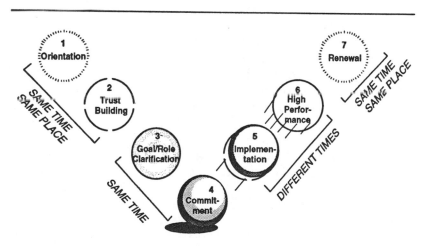

Figure 2.6
Preferred Groupware Options for Team Performance

initial exploration, we used both of these frameworks to ask ourselves, "What groupware options (as suggested by the 4-Square Map) will help yield the greatest group performance (when applied to the stages of the Team Performance Model)?"

At the stages of orientation and trust building, we have found that *same-time/same-place* groupware is critical. When people don't know each other, as in the start of any journey, the immediacy of face-to-face contact is important, along with the qualitative aspects of a nonverbal presence among people. Electronic groupware can play a role in the early stages, but "peopleware" (*same time/same place*) is the most important set of tools to help team members orient themselves and build trust. The emphasis here is on the subtleties and richness of experience in face-to-face meetings, with enhancement—as appropriate—from electronic tools.

When a team moves to the goal/role clarification and commitment stages, however, *same-place* groupware is often unnecessary, especially if a team is well-oriented and shares a level of trust. In today's decentralized, often international, environment, it is often a relief *not* to have to travel. What is needed, however, is quick feedback and lots of cross-checking. In clarifying goals and roles, and in making commitments, it is important to know that one's ideas are heard and to get a quick sense of how people are responding to them. *Same-time groupware* can do this, whether or not all the participants are in the same room. Video or audio teleconferences, for example, allow people to have a synchronous discussion with immediate feedback—but without the need for all the participants to be in the same physical location. Teleconferences can provide a full range of narrative, numeric, and visual communications. Face-to-face meetings are sometimes necessary for final commitments, in a ceremonial yet nonetheless powerful way, though this is not always the case. *Same-time* groupware is mandatory, but it can be either *same place* or *different place*—depending on the circumstances.

After commitments are made, the implementation stage begins—leading to high performance in some cases where groups dedicate themselves to mastering their work, or in others it might be simply getting the job done on time and within budget. Regardless, the demand is for flexibility in communications.

The implementation stage is driven by time concerns, and a busy team will often have trouble assembling itself at any one

Temporary Framework for Cooperation

time. The team members must coordinate their efforts but often do not have time to meet in person. This is even more true at the high-performance stage, where team members are anticipating each other's moves and running at full speed. *Different-time* groupware—such as networked scheduling programs or computer conferencing software—is a big help in such situations. In most cases, the groupware of choice will handle *different times / different places*, but the critical characteristic is *different time*. *Same-place / different-time* groupware may be appropriate if the team has the luxury of being located in the same geographic setting. This is the utility of the team room—a three-dimensional shared "bulletin board" for work in progress.

At the end of a project (or phases, in a longer process), the renewal stage again finds people wanting *same-time / same-place* familiarity and immediacy. The team needs to take stock of where it has been, where it might go, and how its actions connect (or fail to connect) with the larger organization of which it is a part. This is much more than an informational matter. Often, celebration is appropriate and important if a team has succeeded. Sometimes a "funeral" and mourning are in order. Groupware must be sensitive to such needs and is likely to require *same-time/same-place* capabilities.

We have used the 4-Square and Team Performance models as a pair, working with early users of groupware. The models provide a practical pain frame for prospective users to employ when considering their options. Throughout the rest of this book we will use this pair of models frequently as a language to talk about groupware tools and the larger issues of how various tools fit together and can be used by real teams.

References

1. G. DeSanctis and B. Gallupe. "A foundation for the study of group decision support systems." *Management Science* 33 (May 1987):5.

2. Stanley M. Davis. *Future Perfect*. Reading, Mass.: Addison-Wesley Publishing Company, 1987.

3. A. B. Drexler, D. Sibbert, and R. H. Forrester. "The team performance model." *Team Building: Blueprints for Productivity*. W. B. Reddy and K. Jamison (eds.). San Diego, Calif.: National Training Laboratory, Institute for Behavioral Sciences, 1988:46–61; M. R. Weisbord. *Organizational Dianosis*. Reading, Mass.: Addison-Wesley Publishing Company, 1978 (1985 printing); L. P. Bradford, J. R. Gibb, and K. D. Benne. *T-group Theory and Laboratory Method: Innovation in Re-education*. J. Wiley, 1967; A. M. Young. *The Reflexive Universe: Evolution of Consciousness*. New York: Delacorte Press/S. Lawrence, 1976.

4. The Drexler/Sibbet/Forrester Team Performance Inventory is available from Graphic Guides, Inc., in San Francisco and Quality Team Performance, Inc., in North Potomac, Maryland.

3

Groupware Turns Out to Be More than Electronics

The Value of Common Languages and Conceptual Models

How will team cultures integrate and cooperate in the 1990s? For all our emphasis on computers and groupware, the tide of fragmentation and change seems as strong as ever. Office automation still isn't yielding the results everyone wants. The old mainframe cultures didn't anticipate the PCs—no one really did—yet PCs came in like locusts and ate up the existing work culture, agreements, and information systems without any thought as to what would replace them.

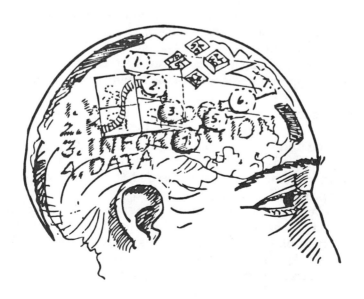

As technologists try solution after solution, hoping that new tools will work some kind of magic, the focus increasingly turns back to the basic unit for all intelligent work, the human brain. Without common frameworks, models, and language, coordination tools can't even be assessed, let alone installed and mastered for results. In this chapter we explore key dimensions of these issues.

Information Flow Shapes Organizations

Decisions about how we handle information lie at the root of how we structure organizations, says Richard Galbraith.[1] He postulates that the need to handle information is a function of how much uncertainty exists in a system. Higher uncertainty means more information must be processed. Lower uncertainty requires less information processing. Decisions about how we process information subsequently form the framework for organizational structures.

The structure of collaborative workgroups also flows from the information they are being asked to process by the organization. And the appropriate structuring mechanisms get chosen after the group understands what it has to do and how often it will have to meet, write, or communicate to do it.

Intuition, augmented with "conceptual tools," is what groups use to make these determinations. At the largest level, these are called world views, or paradigms. It's what every human uses as a basis for acting and thinking. At a more systematized and conscious level, they become models, frameworks for thinking, or meta-languages.

In stable, homogeneous cultures, consistent frameworks become widespread and serve as the foundation for cooperative action. They are generally transparent to the users. An example would be successful engineering cultures after World War II. With a management group possessed of a common language of engineering and a common base experience of war and survival, the teaming and group activity could flourish with a shared operating system. The country needed the goods which these cultures produced, and many prospered.

Today's business environment is searching for such bases of work, largely having lost them since the workforce diversified, technology proliferated, and business began going global and multinational. Candidate operating environments flourish and die. Most large companies are a hodgepodge of tools and language. Sometimes Total Quality provides a big framework, if top management understands it in western cultural terms and can spread the message to others. Sometimes sociotechnical system ideas integrate. But, by and large, discovering these integrating approaches and languages is the challenge of our time.

Meta-Challenges at the Language Level: Learning to Learn

The act of leading effective business teams will, if the Groupware Users' Project is a mirror, plunge both team leaders and participants into the meta-challenge of agreeing on conceptual tools and language systems, if groups are to work at all, let alone be high performing. And managing the companywide implementation and use of conceptual tools and languages will be a competitive differentiator.

More and more companies are realizing that their real capital in today's information age is the ability of their employees to learn. This human capital is different from money or material assets. It actually grows with use. We suspect groupware is that collection of tools which completes an environment where organizational learning and team learning can take place.

At the heart of learning is getting feedback. Humans must see, hear, or sense the results of their actions to learn from them. If the action is communication-related, as much of group work is, the feedback must be provided in ways that can be remembered and compared—if group learning is to flourish. This requires common language and common operating frameworks. These exist in partnership with physical and electronic tools, which are all designed with these shared communication frameworks in mind. In fact, accepting and working with electronic groupware could become a primary way of learning to think and communicate in new ways.

Multilingual Requirements

As English itself becomes more and more global, and meanings begin to proliferate for all the important words, we'll need other languages simply to define basic terms. Numbers already provide one kind of mediating language. Graphics are rapidly emerging as another. Interface environments that are multimedia are yet

GROUP WARE!

INFOTAINMENT

Decision Support Systems

"Groupware is A.I.!"

Dyson

The Learning Org.

Seybold

Metaphor

Room. Ware.

CALS (NMY)

GROUPWARE USERS PROJECT '89

Johansen

IFTF

OBSERVERS

Alsop

"DATA INTERPRETATION" (DIS)

Group Writing

Process Design...

Coordination Theory

Information Refineries

"INFO MATING"

CMI Capture Lab

UNIV. OF MICH.

O ICEMAIL

INFORMATION

E·MAIL

Malone M.I.T.

High Pressure.

INDUSTRIAL WEAKENING

C.M. UNIV. "Andrew"

INFO MAPPING Horn

LOTUS

Media Lab

NATIONAL TRAINING LABS.

Long term climate change.

Simon

Applegate HARVARD

ON TECHNOLOGY

TELEVERKET

socio tech / T.Q.

DEC

BLOCK PETRELLA WEISBORD

High Commitment Work Systems

N.J.I.T. ASTD

IBM

AARHUS UNIV.

Maj.

1992

GLOBALIZATION

INFRASTRUCTURES

Bostons

ISDN

TELECOM

MCC Wagner GTE

UNIV. GEORGIA

?

INFRASTRUCTURES

FAX · SATEL.

TELEPHONY

·CABLE···

1990 for DAVID SIBBET

another. And within these new languages are organizing models and metaphors which are essential for the process of converting data to information. Already some conceptual tools like the Myers–Briggs Type Indicator, the Hersey/Blanchard Situational Leadership Model, and the Blake and Mouton Managerial Grid[2] are becoming standards.

Learning about Commitment

Paradoxically, with choices will come an even greater need for discipline. Emerging theories of process suggest that the types of freedoms we associate with high performance—in the arts, sports, or business—are all products of mastering constraints, not eliminating them. In fact, all systems that exhibit high flexibility and adaptability are built around very critical core elements that are not arbitrary. Jazz requires chord agreements and a beat. Gymnasts rely on supple spines. Overnight delivery companies rely on crack dispatch and transportation control systems. Lobbying groups rely on well-honed computer networks. The Japanese rely on a centuries-deep understanding of customs and communication patterns.

Project teams are not exempt. They adopt groupware only as fast as they can foresee mastering it—and if the group's will to commit is not present, the new tools will be avoided, no matter how promising. All this means that becoming aware of and disciplined about conceptual frameworks and language probably will be a requirement for organizations wanting to utilize groupware fully.

How can businesses make these evaluations? Is there consensus on benefits? What kinds of groupware work the best and where? These are the questions that drove the creation of the Groupware Users' Project.

That groups need some kind of integrating tools is really not debatable. Without integration, a group would not deserve the name "team." But in today's world the integration isn't built in. It must be thought about consciously. It appears that choosing something is better than not facing the choice. And choosing a language or tool that empowers communication about all these issues is beginning to look like a step that, itself, may become fundamental. This book is a step toward marking out such early understandings. It may be that one of the great emerging values of groupware will be to support groups in making these choices of conceptual tools and helping train people in their use.

References

1. J. R. Galbraith. *Designing Complex Organizations*. Reading, Mass.: Addison-Wesley Publishing Company, 1973.

2. I. B. Myers. *The Meyers-Briggs Type Indicator*. Palo Alto, Calif.: Consulting Psychologists Press, 1962; P. Hersey and K. H. Blanchard. *Management of Organizational Behavior* (1st Edition). Englewood Cliffs, N.J.: Prentice-Hall, 1969; R. R. Blake and J. S. Mouton. *The New Managerial Grid*. Houston, Tex.: Gulf, 1978.

Part II
Electronic Tools for Teams

4

Groupware Building Blocks

Electronic Infrastructure

Although many products are now marketed as "groupware," the term embodies a concept much broader than any single technology, software, or product. Groupware is an approach to using the computing and communications tools and infrastructure that already exist in organizations to better support the work of teams and groups. In many cases, simply adding a few new features or showing people a new way of using the tools will allow the organization to get the benefits of groupware.

The basic groupware building blocks are the telephone, the computer, and the conference room. Almost all groupware tools and applications build on this infrastructure. The telephone is the most fundamental electronic groupware building block. It is ubiquitous, well understood, and the best networked groupware terminal available in business. Almost every desktop in the industrialized world has one. Everyone knows how to use it. The computer is the next building block for groupware. It has much more power and versatility than the telephone but is more expensive and more complicated to learn and use. Most groupware product development has gone into making computer applications, particularly for the personal computer. The final building block for groupware is the conference room. It is the site of many meetings for most business groups. For a lot of business teams, it can be thought of as the "groupwhere."

In this chapter we identify the groupware functions that can be built on each of these pieces of organizational infrastructure, and we examine what happens when the infrastructures are combined.

Telephone

The telephone is not merely the most ubiquitous of groupware terminals, it is also the most underused. We perceive the phone as a tool for person-to-person, real-time communication, but it is also an excellent groupware platform. Three major approaches to groupware-by-telephone are commonly used—each one reaches beyond the constraints of person-to-person usage.

The first approach is to turn the telephone from a medium for synchronous person-to-person communication to one for synchronous group communication—teleconferencing. Audio conferencing services and hardware are available that allow as many as scores of users to connect to the same conversation simultaneously. Conferences can be organized so that an operator dials all participants near the scheduled time of the conference. Alternatively, all members can dial a single number and give a conference code that allows them to connect to their meeting (a "meet-me" conference).

A second approach is to add memory; this will allow the telephone to be used asynchronously. Secretaries and receptionists have been taking messages for as long as the telephone has been in business use. Voice mail does just that electronically. At its simplest, it acts as an electronic answering machine. Most voice mail systems have additional features that allow them to be used by groups as groupware. These include the ability to address messages to a distribution list, to forward messages, and to include "carbon copies." Voice mail systems also can be hooked to other communication devices, such as pagers, to alert team members that an urgent message is waiting.

The last approach is to use the telephone as an information tool rather than as a communication tool. Voice response (or audiotex) tools allow information to be stored and retrieved using a standard touchtone keypad. The system offers or asks for information by a series of recorded (or synthesized) voice prompts. The user navigates with keypad responses that allow him or her either to hear recorded information or to leave structured, recorded messages.

Computer

Computers are at the core of much groupware activity. Personal computers have reached a significant penetration of desktops in business. A growing number are being linked into local area networks (LANs). A whole range of software and network products have been introduced that use the personal computer as the *interpersonal* computer.

The simplest groupware application of the computer infrastructure—individual use in support of the group—entails no networking at all. This involves between-meeting preparation of text, spreadsheets, graphics, and other material that is used by the group. The material may be presented in an electronic form or, more commonly, on paper.

More significant group work occurs when computer infrastructures are networked. A networked system allows electronic connections—and thus communication and information flow—that reflect the organizational structure of the team. A common computer network infrastructure is electronic mail. Like the telephone, electronic mail is oriented primarily toward person-to-person communication. It simulates the flow of paper notes, memos, and letters in an organization, but it can be a stepping stone to groupware functions. Just as with voice mail, the first step is the use of group distribution lists. They allow users to communicate the same message to any number of users.

Distribution lists allow the communication of information to reflect a group's structure, but they don't help with ways information is stored and retrieved. Computer conferencing allows the group to keep a structured memory ordered by time, by topic, by contributor, or in any other way, of all exchanges by the group. The exchanges can be structured and organized as they are created, giving a sense of order to the group's communications. The conference provides a roadmap of the group's thinking and a common reference point.

The uses of electronic mail and conferencing differ according to the size of the group involved. Person-to-person uses action as a replacement for notes and memos. Small groups and teams of up to 20 people make the best use of conferencing as a tool for coordinating their work across locations and parts of the enterprise. It is well used to accelerate sequential work under a time deadline. Larger groups can use conferencing as a way to coordinate diffuse efforts under a single umbrella and keeping a wider constituency informed of developments.

Local area networks (LANs) are often used in two ways: (1) to give people on the network shared access to costly resources such as printers, high-speed modems, software programs, and large-scale storage; and (2) to give them shared access to files. The second aspect is of most interest for groupware. By having common access to files, members of a team can work on the same documents. Software products are available that facilitate such sharing, including group writing and editing tools, shared screen software, and project management tools.

Some companies are linking many LANs into an enterprisewide network—a network of networks. These networks combine the advantages of local networks—local control and maintenance, responsive service, and relatively easy expandability—with the universal electronic mail access, companywide standardization of software, and economical use of very costly resources of mainframe systems.

Conference Room

Conference rooms are where teams do much of their work as groups. At its most basic a conference room requires a table and enough chairs for all participants. Additional equipment may be present in the conference room, including flip charts, whiteboards, copyboards, and overhead and slide projectors.

Bringing the Computer Into the Conference Room

A central role of groupware is to support the work of teams in face-to-face meetings. Many applications are premised on bringing the capabilities of computers into the conference room, including the display of work prepared ahead of time by computer, the ability to share personal data with others, or the use of computer processing power—all during the meeting. Computers remain a novelty in conference rooms, but the spread of portables is showing some of the advantages of using computers there. In the future, we expect to see more computers permanently installed in conference rooms.

The simplest use of computers in conference rooms is as a display tool for information prepared ahead of time. Two kinds of devices hook to the output of the computer—simple liquid crystal diode (LCD) plates that display the screen when set atop an overhead projector, and three-color (RGB) video projectors that turn the output into a video signal. These same devices can be used to display notes taken during the meeting by a recorder or facilitator, just as a whiteboard or a copyboard would be used—with the added advantage that everyone can leave the meeting with a freshly printed set of notes.

When decision support software is used, the computer in the conference room can become a more active "participant" in meetings. This type of software ranges from simple decision support packages that help structure a group's thinking about a problem to more complex systems that include polling and instant feedback, and can facilitate meetings that must produce decisions. The quality of decisions may improve because the software pushes participants to structure a decision that would have been made ad hoc. Or the software may help separate the merits of different positions from the persuasiveness of their proponents by depersonalizing the decision process. Also, it may be easier for people to accept a decision that differs from their own opinions because the decision is (or seems) more objective.

A computer in the conference room gains even more power when it is hooked to the network that is used throughout the organization. If a company has a LAN with common data servers, all participants in a conference can have access to their data without having to limit themselves to what they can bring on a diskette.

The most elaborate forms of room-based groupware place a workstation at every seat in the conference room. The workstations are connected locally and to the larger network. Specialized group software is available that permits the group to integrate brainstorming, idea organization, ranking and voting, and decision support—a complete electronic meeting system.

Bringing the Telephone Into the Conference Room

Telephones are somewhat more common in conference rooms than computers. Although telephones too often are used as a distraction from the meeting, they also have groupware uses. Telephones in conference rooms allow a meeting to happen in different places at the same time, expanding the geographic scope of the team. The addition of a speakerphone can bring a single external expert or participant into the meeting. If there are speakerphones on both sides of a conversation, an audio teleconference between two groups becomes practical. Other communications media can be added to the core of a telephone in a conference room to fill out the range of sides of the conversation; thus an audio teleconference between two groups becomes practical. Fax machines can be used for exchanging documents. More elaborate communications media can be added to the core of a telephone in a conference room to fill out the range of teleconferencing approaches. By connecting two computers over the phone line, participants can exchange computer screens and documents during the meeting. By adding a graphics system, they can transmit drawings and other visual ideas. Television cameras and high-bandwidth communication lines permit the use of video teleconferencing.

Groupware Building Blocks

Telephone

Telephone
Speakerphone
Audio teleconferencing
   services
Voice mail
Audiotex

Computer

Personal computers
Local area networks
Wide area networks
Electronic mail
Computer conferencing

Conference room

Flip charts
Whiteboards
Copyboards
Overhead and slide
   projectors

Computers in the conference room

PC projectors
Group decision support
Local area network links
Integrated group software

Communications in the conference room

Telephones/Speakerphones
Audiographics
Video teleconferencing
Facsimile

Computers and telephones

Electronic mail
Electronic and voice mail
   links

Many interesting groupware applications are based on combining the basic building blocks—telephone, computer, and conference room—into links or hybrids.

Linking the Telephone to the Computer

Use of a telephone in concert with a personal computer gives members of a team much wider geographic access to people and information. Instead of limiting electronic mail to a single premise, it can be reached from any telephone line. Members of a team can be located anywhere and can do much of their work asynchronously using electronic mail. Users also can get access

I said, "I'm glad they provided a low-tech backup for a high-tech system."

to computer conferencing from wherever they are. Thus they can carry on a meeting without worrying about geographic or time factors.

We discovered in our research that groups tend to be heavy users of electronic mail, or heavy users of voice mail, but not both. When a group is composed of mixed users, there may be a cultural gap that causes people to miss messages in one medium or another. In fact, one of the most commonly reported problems in using electronic mail is that infrequent users don't pick up their messages often enough and are out of touch with the work of the group. Linking the telephone to the computer can help bridge that gap. When the telecommunications system is run on a computer that is compatible or can communicate with the electronic-mail computer, it is possible to give voice-mail notification of electronic-mail messages and electronic-mail notification of voice-mail messages. Some systems are even available that will "read" an electronic-mail message over the phone in a synthesized voice. (The opposite service—converting free-form voice messages to printed text—is not available and is at least several years away.)

5

Electronic Mail

*A Surprisingly Powerful
Groupware Platform*

Though groupware remains in its infancy, users of electronic mail (E-mail) and computer conferencing (text messaging for groups via keyboards) have wasted no time in developing their own unique culture.

- The medium is completely self-activated—people must be motivated to log on and collect their messages. Participants in an E-mail exchange assume that everyone logs on regularly and keeps up to date. Consequently, they have little patience for the excuse that one missed the message because one didn't log on.

- It is perfectly acceptable in many systems (particularly those used by technical people) to "flame" on any topic. Flames are strongly worded opinions on everything from the latest system upgrade to the latest baseball scores. Many conferences stop short of ad hominem attacks, but even they are fair game in others. "Flaming" is a leftover from the university environments in which computer conferencing began.

- Other (mainly corporate) systems have developed social norms, most of which are very polite. One firm, in fact, encourages users not to send a response to electronic mail immediately. Instead, they are asked to compose a response when they want but to hold it overnight. In the fresh light of morning, many messages are seen to be

```
:)   smile

:(   frown

;)   wink

:^   tongue in cheek
```

Figure 5.1

unnecessary or inappropriate. This has the side benefit of holding down overall mail volume.

- The inherent lack of expressiveness (how does one grin in a typed message?) in a messaging system has not stifled human expression and creativity. A whole symbolic language has evolved on conferencing systems. For example, the users of one system have developed the symbology shown in Fig. 5.1.

The bottom line is that ingenuity will always conspire to overcome the limitations of any communications medium. In fact, organizations can benefit by cultivating these sorts of solutions.

6

Voice Mail

Four Phases of User Behavior

Voice mail (store-and-forward telephone messaging) is emerging as an important groupware tool. In general, voice-mail systems are selling well, and user acceptance is quite positive. However, in the course of our work in the last few years, we have begun to notice curious patterns in acceptance by specific groups. For example, some organizations that are enthusiastic users of E-mail have reacted with indifference to voice mail. In other cases, the opposite is true. But the one common denominator in all of the success stories is a peculiar pattern of user acceptance—a four-step process that moves from avoidance to full use of voice mail as a true groupware tool. Here is what we discovered.

Phase 1: Avoidance

The first reaction to encountering a voice mail box is to hang up on it. People feel uncomfortable leaving their voices on tape and are afraid that they'll sound stupid. The increased probability of running into home answering machines is beginning to soften them up. The first-time owner of a voice mail box is often reluctant to record a greeting, and will rely on the system's default greeting.

Phase 2: Electronic *"While You Were Out . . ."*

The second reaction to encountering a voice mail box is to leave a simple message giving name, number, and when to call back. Most users still aren't comfortable enough with the technology to leave lengthy or substantive messages. Similarly, the owner of the box will leave a simple, general-purpose outgoing message and will not change it.

Phase 3: Asynchronous Communication

The third phase in acceptance of voice mail is to leave substantive messages that refer to the business at hand and to other messages that have been exchanged in the past. At this point, individuals begin to benefit from communicating anywhere, anytime. The owner of the box begins to make use of more advanced functions, including recording alternative outgoing messages during vacations or travel.

Phase 4: Groupware

In the fourth phase of using voice mail as groupware, people use the full power of advanced functions. The voice mail system becomes a tool that can be tailored to fit each team in which a person participates. Functions such as distribution lists, message confirmation, and audiotex menuing can be used to connect users more closely to the group. Voice mail can be linked with other technologies to achieve more group power. Examples include linking voice mail to pagers to notify users of incoming messages, using voice-mail group distribution lists to announce a "meet me if you can" audio teleconference, and giving voice-mail notification of electronic-mail messages. The owner of a voice mail box can give other people access to certain messages through guest, secretary, and personal privileges.

7

Team-Room Design

Checklist for a Decision-Support Room

As businesses have moved more and more to team-based work, team rooms have come to be a central device for organizing their work. The norm has been for people in workstations and small offices (often in areas with space dividers) to use one or more available conference rooms for team meetings. In this chapter we

suggest some specifications to consider when designing a team room.

One of the assumptions we are making is that as technological options increase, the designer will want to move more and more toward completely flexible room environments that function more like small theaters than command centers. Fixed-design rooms, as a rule, do not serve as usefully over time as modular ones. In some ways, a team room is like a three-dimensional analog of the team's work. The more flexibly it can reflect agreements about the structure and function of the team, the more it will support rather than encumber a working group.

Flexible Furniture

Teams have many different purposes. One cannot presume that each will be run like a board meeting in need of a long table. In fact, the act of setting up a team room can be a key team-building and focusing activity. Team rooms should have small, modular tables that can be arranged in many configurations. Seating also should be flexible. Overly bulky, comfortable chairs are not ideal.

Teams frequently like to work at round or oval tables that allow enough space for one side of the room to function as a display wall. Teams need multiple inputs, and this is facilitated when everyone can see each other and the presentation materials easily.

A flexible team room would be large enough to have modular tables that could pull apart to enable several small groups to meet at once, if necessary. Most workgroups range from 2 to 15 people. Above that size, groups break down into smaller teams anyway. A flexible team room would be useful to such smaller units and could still double as a conference room for larger groups.

Smooth Walls

The most important thing that happens in a team room is communication. Smooth wall surfaces make it easy to hang charts and paper that can be used to create interactive—and productive—visual displays. Most teams make intensive use of such displays and prefer to use walls that accept masking tape so that the paper doesn't rip down as it does with push-pins.

An ideal room would have one wall that allowed both pinning—for example, for prepared drawings like those architects and designers make for presentation—and taping. A self-healing material over a relatively soft undersurface that accepts push-pins is best and affords the flexibility needed for various team communication strategies.

Lighting

Flexible lighting is very useful. It is most important to have the walls that are working surfaces well lit. Some groups take Polaroids of charts as a working record. This works best with even wall lighting.

Rooms with fluorescent lighting may be extremely taxing to work in for long periods because its strobing and partial frequencies strain the eyes. Full spectrum lights help, but the best lighting is natural light. Team rooms should be on the outside perimeter of buildings to have at least one wall of windows. It is helpful to have dimming features that take into account overhead projection. This allows some room lights to remain on.

Whiteboards

Most team rooms contain whiteboards. These are very useful and are good for attaching paper as well, if a team wants to keep its work. As multiple teams use team rooms, having a stash of displays that can reorient members will be important, and working on paper will persist in being an important aspect of team work.

Flip-Chart Stands

Even with whiteboards, flip charts are invaluable. The paper can be used flat on the table or on the stands. It can easily be put into a copyboard and copied. A team room should have enough room for several chart stands, while still allowing room for tables and chairs.

Copyboards

Blackboard-sized copyboards are now becoming common in conference rooms. Of the dozen or so varieties, only a few use scanner bars, thereby allowing charts and paper displays to be copied easily.

TEAM ROOM

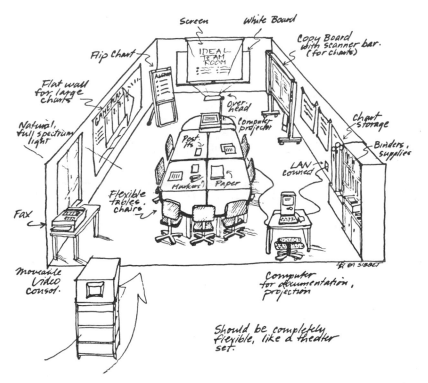

These are far and away the most useful and flexible. The copyboards that use erasable mylar are designed for working groups that do not need to keep all their displays up at the same time, because the smaller versions are sufficient. This is simply not the case for complex planning projects, for which an entire room may become a visual environment that supports systems thinking at a group level. The scanner bar copyboards provide for both options.

The ability to provide small copies of large displays is a popular productivity tool for many groups. Some of the copyboard's helpful applications are recording action items, schedules, key models, and frameworks that the group is using to guide its activity.

Eventually these boards should provide a direct feed into a computer, thereby allowing digital replays of the conceptual graphics that come out of design sessions as well as communication to different places.

Chart and Supply Storage

If more than one team intends to use a room, each will need storage to keep the charts and displays that are critical to its work. Two types of storage are needed: one to hold flip-chart displays and perhaps the chart stands themselves, and one to allow for long, rolled-up displays. Storage cubes like those for architects' drawings would work well. A team will also have other key materials to store. Something resembling lockers might become a feature in rooms with high multiple use.

Flexible Electric Outlets and LANs

Increasingly, teams will use interactive computers and projectors for their work, along with the more traditional overheads. Designers should assume that computers might end up in any part of the room, and outlets should be easily accessible. It would be useful to provide a LAN for workgroups that want to link up temporarily in the course of an intense planning session.

Desktop Publishing and Computer Projection Capability

A deluxe team room would have a desktop computer system and laser printer set up for action, as well as a projection capability. Once a team has passed the creative stages of its work, preparation of presentations and reports is greatly facilitated by working directly on documents that can be printed out. Many team facilitators work directly with computer outline and drawing programs to record group contributions to a session. Such stations could be available on carts, much like audio-visual equipment, and reservable if resources are thin.

Screens

Flexible stand-up screens are preferable to fixed screens in a team room, because it is difficult to predict all the different kinds of arrangements teams might want to try. Screens are critical for overheads, projected computers, and film.

Access to Copiers

Copiers should be close to team rooms. Making multiple reproductions and creating presentation copies is integral to the work of most contemporary teams.

A Preferred Scenario

The most general-purpose, flexible arrangement for a team room would be a square to rectangular shape that allows for a modular table arrangement, computer display off to one side, a long whiteboard wall in front with about 15 feet of display space, and a copyboard off to the other side. One wall would let in natural light, and the other walls would allow for easy hanging of large paper display sheets. Such a room would let a workgroup flexibly represent all their communications at the macro level of the wall or the micro level of the table.

The most ideal situation for a team would be to have a room dedicated to its activities. In the days before books, teachers would create "memory theaters" because of the strong relationship some people have to spatial memory. A team meeting in the same room can literally pick up where it left off as its members reorient themselves to the visual information left on display.

*"It's portable roomware. Not only does it travel . . .
but we're also going to enter it as a float in the Rose
Bowl Parade."*

A dedicated room is also a statement of the organizational importance of the team relative to its task. Such a room becomes, in a sense, a simulation of whatever problem, product, or system a team is working on—a virtual laboratory.

Eventually, team rooms will become a node in the larger organizational information system, with all data files accessible through special display ports. In the meantime, paper, markers, copyboards, and copiers must provide the necessary links within and outside of meetings.

8

Hooked on Electronic Copyboards

Quick, Inexpensive, and Easy-to-Use Groupware

An electronic copyboard is one of the best low-tech team aids around. It's an easy-to-use, relatively inexpensive, group memory device; any time spent working visually will help clarify objectives or foster commitment, and a copyboard can help. With an electronic copyboard, teams can reduce note-taking and transcribing time and instead capture crea-

tive ideas once and for all. All team members can take away a copy of exactly the same material, with all the memories of the meeting and the process that the copy evokes. Saved transcription costs even can "pay" for a copyboard. (Of course, you can argue that there is some value in having the transcribed information in electronic form.) Cost aside, electronic copyboards also can save time and reduce hassles.

Still, many electronic copyboards sit blank during meetings. It turns out that group leaders and members don't know how to use them, physically or conceptually. Physical use is relatively easy (see the "Techniques" box). Conceptual use in meetings takes a bit of attention to the beginning, middle, and end of group processes. Meetings have known opening moves. You should first inform meeting attendees why they are there by

Techniques for Using Electronic Copyboards

Try it before the meeting to test how it works. Some electronic copyboards have multiple blank frames that wrap around inside the board (typically two or four frames). Others have a single face, with a copying device that scans the face. If yours has multiple faces, reset the copyboard at the first frame unless the copyboard has an endless loop of frames. Also, erase all the frames—after making a copy of them, just in case.

Make sure you've got all the necessary supplies. Check to see if you have a full roll of copy paper and know where to get a back-up supply. You'll also need an eraser and special markers.

Use the right kind of markers. Use "dry erase" markers only. (If, however, you use a nonerase marker, you can clean up the marks by inking over them with a dry-erase pen, erasing as you go. Try it—it's magic.)

Use marker colors that copy well. Black and blue work best; yellow, orange, brown, and red do not work well. None of the available copyboards copies color yet, so your copies will not show color differences.

Manage your space. Start on the left of frames to get the most out of your space. Start on frame 1 if you have multiple frames. If you use multiple frames at the same time, switching back and forth between them to record different topics, you'll have to remember "what's on second." Number and date your originals.

Post one copy of every frame recorded on the wall. It's a good idea to keep a master copy. Furthermore, it's nice to have a chronology of copies that reflects the movement of the meeting.

posting an agenda and a list of expected outcomes. Then, if attendees don't all know each other, you can draw a square or circle to denote the table, and write down each person's name, showing her or his location around the table.

You can't always predict what kind of visuals you'll need during the middle of the meeting. Be prepared to capture the creative development of ideas. In one case, a group of divisional marketing managers with whom we worked argued over how many people and how much of the advertising budget they would need from each division to introduce a new product line that had components from all divisions. Eventually, they created a matrix of components down the vertical axis, and people, budget, and primary owners across the horizontal axis. The group worked for hours to get the right mix of people and dollars. When they were finished, the division directors signed their names, showing their commitment of financial and human resources.

At the end of the meeting, you can use the copyboard to record anything that needs to be reinforced—action lists, decision logs, and implementation plans. With multiple-frame copyboards, one frame of the copyboard can be used to record an action list and another to record key decisions generated during a meeting. Some teams that pay attention to improving their group process use the copyboard to record "what works" and "what can be improved" lists.

Professional meeting facilitators argue over which copyboards work best (see the "Features to Look For" box). Some like the multiple-frame boards. They prefer to record on a medium where they can draft/erase/redraft/erase, etc., to refine their lists or graphics. Other facilitators prefer to use flip charts and wall graphics as their primary group memory. They like the single-face copyboard (which also can be used to record material) with an overhead scanner bar. One group, for example, cut large rolls of blank newsprint (using a giant bandsaw) to fit the copyboard so that their large displays could be copied easily.

A new variation on the electronic copyboard theme is a digital camera. This is a briefcase-sized portable image copier with a built-in thermal printer. You can point and shoot an image of a blackboard, whiteboard, flip chart, or projected overhead transparency, or even take a team image.

Electronic Copyboard Features to Look For

- Easy to "walk up and use"
- Good quality output
- Top bar scanner to copy flip charts or newsprint, or direct access to frames (multiple-frame copyboards)
- Ability to copy multiple frames on a single copy

- Ability to copy requested frames (frame 1 only, or frames 1 and 4, etc.)
- Background suppressor (filters out marker "chalk marks")
- Multiple paper sizes (8 ½ by 11, and 8 ½ by 20 for multiple-frame copies)
- Easily transportable (unless you can afford one for each of your meeting rooms)
- Sheet-fed plain paper (Wouldn't it be nice not to have thermal paper?)
- Remote control (for us lazy leaders)

9

TQ Groupware

Watch for Total Quality Software

A likely market development to watch for will be the emergence
of groupware software that supports and delivers Total Quality
(TQ) programs. Thus TQ Groupware could become one of the first
really new product classes to emerge in the groupware
marketplace.

Quality improvement programs are on the rise in large
U.S. companies, as well as internationally. The most dramatic
success stories have come from Japan (and, to a lesser extent,
Germany). Typically, such programs consist of widespread train-

ing geared toward a whole-company approach to quality improvement. There are many names for such efforts, including TQC (Total Quality Control), TQ (Total Quality), and QIP (Quality Improvement Program). The roots of these programs track to W. Edwards Deming, Joseph Juran, and others.[1]

The defining characteristics of TQ programs boil down to

- focus on customers,
- enterprisewide view,
- emphasis on process, rather than outcomes,
- decisions driven by data,
- specialized techniques for data analysis, and
- long-term orientation.

Our estimate is that perhaps 30% of the *Fortune* 500 companies have large-scale quality programs under way and that about 50% have significant trials or portions of their businesses with active TQ efforts.

In Japan, quality programs typically involve heavy use of business teams or quality circles. Surprisingly, however, Japanese quality teams rarely use electronic tools. From discussions that we have had with experts on Japan, we have found that quality methods seem to be so ingrained in Japanese business practices that new electronic tools just are not considered. Also, Japanese business practices put such an emphasis on interpersonal relationships that the use of electronic tools for team work may seem unnatural or inappropriate.

American companies definitely lag behind Japan on the TQ front. Also, American companies do not have Japan's rich history of working with business teams. American teams, however, seem quite open to using electronic tools. It is possible that American teams may be able to leapfrog Japanese teams by using electronic groupware to improve quality.

For example, Ford Motor Company has developed its own software program to support the creation and modification of the "House of Quality," a specific quality technique for problem identification, problem prevention, and market or vehicle planning. This software development effort is part of a general move by Ford into the area of Quality Function Deployment (QFD), which they view as a system for translating customer demands into products. At Ford, a team of 8 to 12 people meets in a room with a PC, a PC projection system, and perhaps an overhead projector operated by a "scribe." The participants come from varied backgrounds, such as planning, styling, marketing, product development, purchasing, manufacturing, assembly, and engineering. Specific product attributes are discussed and agreed upon, at which time they are added to the group-authored House of Quality. A graphic summary display is developed, discussed, and revised by the group.

A typical QFD process at Ford will take 3 to 12 months to complete. The completed House of Quality provides an excellent graphic summary of many variables considered by the group. The electronic groupware allows the group to develop the House of Quality and see it as it goes up. More importantly, modifications can be made, and the overall diagram (which can become quite complex) can be redrawn quickly by the software program. In Japan, the House of Quality graphic is typically drawn and redrawn by an artist, which takes time and money. Ford claims shorter product development cycles, fewer problems during production, and better fulfillment of consumer needs through use of the QFD process. The company is now considering the possibility of making the software commercially available, or at least available to its suppliers.

Another approach to TQ Groupware is "CFMpro" (Technology and Strategy Group, Cambridge, Massachusetts), a software tool designed to support what is referred to in Japan as the product development process (PDP). It utilizes networks, workstation capabilities for analysis, X-Window features, and versatile communications software to facilitate the product development process through its various stages. This tool is designed for use by cross-functional teams; it provides a common framework within which a diverse team can work. CFMpro forces the user to think top-down, as is typical of most TQ processes. (Most of today's project management tools force the user to think bottom-up, from specific dates and tasks.) In CFMpro, milestones and schedules are tracked, but with constant reminders regarding the overall process that is under way. CFMpro positions itself as a "road map" to various online data available to the team. This software can be used either in a team room or over a network. It is currently developed in C in a Macintosh environment, but the developers are exploring X-Window options and other possible development environments.

A final example is the IBM Decision Conference Centers. These rooms, discussed elsewhere in this book, have workstations for each participant and software designed to assist a group in its various activities. At IBM, the Decision Centers have been used on an experimental basis for implementation of Total Quality techniques. The Decision Center process is introduced in mandatory training sessions on specific aspects of Total Quality, as practiced at IBM. The software tools (developed at the University of Arizona) are all adaptable for use in a TQ context: electronic brainstorming, idea organization, stakeholder analysis, development of parallel ideas or threads, and voting. The facilitator (a vital part of the use of the centers) brings most of the specific TQ content and procedures to the meeting, and the software is employed for TQ purposes.

For example, groups can brainstorm answers to questions like, "What are we doing now that we should not be doing?" Once a list of items is developed, it can be rated or ranked in terms of potential impacts on time utilization, money, and quality. The results of such sessions can be shared across levels as the TQ process is implemented. At later sessions, other questions can be considered, such as, "What are we doing as a project that we could be doing better?" The experience from these initial experiments has been very positive. Major areas of savings have been uncovered that have far surpassed the cost of actually conducting the sessions in the Decision Centers.

These are only three examples of what we feel is an emerging trend. We have said earlier in this book that groupware is more a perspective on telecommunications and computing than it is a new class of products. However, there will be specific classes of groupware products geared toward particular user audiences. We think TQ Groupware will be one of them.

Why? Because TQ programs are a major wave of change in the United States. Implementing these programs with business teams is challenging and often difficult. Groupware can help ease the pains of introducing such programs and can help make them effective once they are in place. There is an obvious need here, a need that has not been met at the present time. TQ Groupware is not an example of a technology looking for a problem to solve. Rather, it is a case of a compelling user need waiting for someone to introduce a groupware solution.

References

1. W.E. Deming. *Out of the Crisis.* Cambridge, Mass.:
   Massachusetts Institute of Technology, Center for
   Advanced Engineering Study, 1988; J.M. Juran (ed.)
   Quality Control Handbook. New York: McGraw-Hill,
   1974; P.B. Crosby. *Quality is Free: The Art of Making
   Quality Certain.* New York: Mentor Books, 1979; See
   also J. Cullen and J. Hollingum. *Implementing Total
   Quality.* Bedford, UK: IFS Publications, Ltd., 1987.

10

ISDN and Groupware

A Future Groupware Platform

 Conventional data communications—communications occurring at relatively low data rates of 9600 bits per second and below with relatively continuous transmissions—are well served by today's data communication services. However, future groupware applications will push communication needs beyond the capabilities these services can offer. For example, bit-mapped screen sharing, integrated voice and data communications, bulk data exchanges for complex shared workspaces, and video conferencing all will require high-speed services. Very "bursty" communications such as the interactive transactions of a group of securities traders or the moves of planners in a real-time simulation game will require much faster connection times than dial-up data communications provide. And interconnected local area networks (LANs) will generate traffic that is both bursty and speed-intensive.

Satisfying those communication needs today is complex and expensive. Users must build customized data communication networks, and some applications are simply impossible to realize. LANs provide virtually instantaneous connections for data communications locally. Interconnecting LANs in a way that preserves this instantaneousness is difficult. Typically it requires customized software and trade-offs between the transmission speed, connection speed, and cost of dial-up—and dedicated lines are unavoidable. Video teleconferencing systems require a high-bandwidth network to be in place. The choices are proliferating by the month—which carrier to use, how much to do in-house, new equipment, new services, switched 56, T-1, Direct Digital Service, T-3, Centrex, etc.

All of these networks are costly to install and to operate. Once installed, they are inflexible and difficult to reconfigure. And the challenges go beyond technology. As companies use different groupware applications that require different types of networks, the administrative overhead and complexity multiply. Many organizations now have formal telecommunications departments, which increasingly have formal links with (or are part of) information systems departments.

ISDN—the Integrated Services Digital Network—has been held out as a standard that can resolve much of this brewing complexity. It is a standard for digital communication over existing installed voice lines. All communications—voice and data—are carried in a digital form from end to end. Devices such as modems (to connect computers over analog phone lines) and codecs (modems for digital video signals) are unnecessary.

The basic ISDN service incorporates two 64 kbps channels and a 16 kbps signalling channel into every telephone line. This is ample capacity for simultaneous data and voice use. A larger scale "primary" ISDN service incorporates twenty-three 64 kbps channels, which can be allocated dynamically to fit user demands.

Benefits of ISDN

Voice/Data Integration

ISDN's primary advantage in groupware applications lies in the fact that all communications—voice, video, data, graphics—are transmitted via a digital form. This allows simultaneous voice and data communications (shared computer screens at the same time as a voice conversation) and makes it possible to integrate voice and data at a deeper level. Digital voice annotations, for example, can be embedded in text documents. An electronic-mail message can be programmed to trigger a voice call notifying the recipient of the message.

Higher Data Rates

Many groupware applications require data communication between remote locations. Today, that communication is typically done using dial-up phone lines and modems that run at speeds of 1200 to 4800 bps. The cost of higher-speed modems is dropping but still remains high. Even if high-speed modems are available at a low cost, speed remains a limitation because most phone lines are not clean enough to support communication faster than 19,200 bps. ISDN will make multiple lines of 64 kbps capacity available.

Faster Connection Times

Dial-up communications require a certain amount of time to seize a dial tone, compose the number, and make the connection—five seconds is a practical lower limit. Applications that require faster responses must either hold the line a long time or be shifted to a dedicated leased line. ISDN will make connections as rapidly as a dedicated line operating through a packet switch.

Local Area Network Bypass

Because all locations that subscribe to ISDN will be available with rapid connections, ISDN can be used in place of a LAN. The members of a group can send data among themselves just as they would on a LAN. Moreover, the same degree of connectivity can be enjoyed by group members at remote sites. ISDN can help create a LAN that is independent of geography—a metropolitan or even a wide area network. A team can have its own team network—no matter where its members are—provided they all have access to ISDN service.

ISDN Signalling Features

The signalling channel of ISDN adds many features that can be built into groupware systems. For example, ISDN can forward the calling number along with the call. Sales representatives calling to upload their sales information to the group's central system from cellular ISDN phones (still far in the future) could be routed directly to the appropriate part of the system without having to enter identification codes. The system could pass them electronic and voice mail automatically. The same information can be used for enhanced system security, for creating closed user groups on public systems, and for determining where to route and forward calls.

Barriers to ISDN

Despite the advantages of ISDN, it will not be used immediately in commercial groupware applications. Barriers remain to its widespread use.

A World of Other Standards

ISDN is but one among many communication standards. It is more encompassing than most and has received wide support, but much uncertainty remains. ISDN cannot become an "island" separate from a sea of other already established standards. For example, terminal manufacturers cannot ignore standards such as X.25 and SNA simply because ISDN has arrived.

Limited Service Availability

ISDN is available only in a minuscule number of markets today. As of 1990, five of the seven Regional Bell Operating Companies have completed or are conducting ISDN trials. One or two of them, along with AT&T, offer the service commercially. Before ISDN can ever begin to meet the needs of most business teams, the service will have to be available at least in most metropolitan areas—and that is at least three to five years off.

Limited Availability of Terminal Equipment

The second wave of ISDN "desksets" has hit the market. They are highly functional—but costly and complex. Typical ISDN terminals—called "desksets"—resemble a personal computer more than they resemble a telephone. Industry wags eagerly note that it is necessary to read the deskset manual just to answer the phone. A common approach is to package the terminal as an add-on card for a personal computer. Many such terminals were shown at the spring 1989 International Telecommunications Association convention—but these devices will remain scarce for several years to come.

Existing Communications Software Performs Poorly with ISDN

The bulk of existing communications software programs cannot communicate over ISDN. The ISDN "command set" is the primary missing element. But even if a software package supports ISDN commands, other incompatibilities and inefficiencies are likely to remain. Most communication software does extensive error checking and flow control—time-consuming steps required for communications on relatively poor-quality analog phone lines. ISDN is a cleaner, faster, already digital environment that includes error checking and flow control, so these steps are unnecessary impediments to rapid transmission. An additional wrinkle is packet size; most communication software sends information in packets of 128 or 256 bytes. ISDN is best suited for much longer packets and operates very inefficiently with these shorter packets.

Although the potential advantages of ISDN are many, we do not believe that it will have a major near-term effect on groupware developments. Computer-based groupware will continue to be developed primarily for LAN and electronic-mail environments until ISDN is more widely available. Voice-based groupware tools will continue to straddle the digital and analog worlds. And video will continue to require costly dedicated lines at transmission rates above 384 kbps.

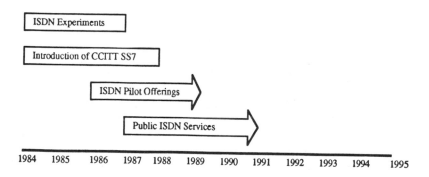

ISDN Is Being Introduced Over a Period of Time.

11

Groupware Applications of Broadband ISDN

Scenarios of a Distant Groupware Nirvana

What lies beyond ISDN?[1] Users will all too rapidly hit the bandwidth limitations of basic ISDN once it is introduced. Although users will get by with the bandwidth of the "primary rate interface" (1.54 Mbps), everyone will clamor for more.

Broadband ISDN is one answer. It is a digital network that runs at 135 Mbps and above—the equivalent of over 2100 basic ISDN channels. Such wide bandwidth is capable of carrying broadcast-quality television without any signal compression. At the modest compression of 2 to 1 (equivalent to 45 Mbps), it can carry three broadcast-quality signals.

What does this mean for groupware? Perhaps this is best shown in the two examples that follow.

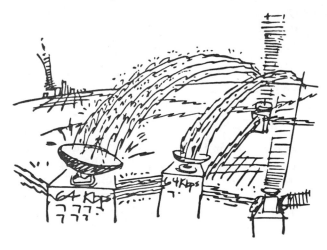

Scenario 1: "Audio Space"

This scenario demonstrates hi-fi binaural audio with high-resolution document scanning, high-speed video still imaging, and high-resolution color screen sharing. Hi-fi binaural audio delivers the illusion of sitting in a virtual "audio space": The voices of the participants come from different directions, as if they were sitting around a conference room table together. The scenario that follows describes a final review of a one-page color glossy advertisement to be placed in a national magazine. The communications link is between several sites at a manufacturing company and at the company's advertising agency.

> The scene opens in an ad agency, with the image of an agency creative director sitting at a workstation with a headset on. (Storyboards are on the walls, along with sample products and generally wild displays; this agency is used to designing flashy ads and commercials.) The director is talking with several other people, who are not present in the same room.

> "I just finished what I hope is the final cut at this one-pager. Are you guys there?" Binaural audio is used here as people introduce themselves; each voice seems to be coming from a different part of the room. About six people are on-line—one from corporate advertising, one from product development, one from legal, the brand manager and assistant brand manager, plus the creative director at the agency. The participants in the meeting go "around the table" informally, each saying a few words of introduction as they go.

> "Take a look at this shot, folks . . . " the creative director says as a color image of the company's product appears on his workstation. Reactions come in via audio: "Wow!" "You're getting close now!" And so on.

> A voice comes from the "other side of the table" via binaural: "I get bogged down in this part of the page, Marty . . . " (Pointer appears on the screen, circling an area of the image containing a line-art illustration—that portion is then highlighted on the screen by color shading. Movement on the screen indicates synchronization of screens back

and forth.) Discussion of that part of the ad continues briefly, reflecting both binaural and high-resolution screen-sharing capabilities.

Scene shifts to second workstation. At this point, another voice comes on and the workstation we have been looking at darkens just as the other one lights up. We see the assistant brand manager sitting at her workstation, in another city and in a very different corporate environment. The audience recognizes a voice that they have heard talking earlier via binaural. "I'm concerned that your ad looks an awful lot like the one that Racor (a competitor) just ran in *Saturday Review* (another magazine). Have you seen that?" When the others say no, the assistant brand manager scans a page from the *Saturday Review* with a hand-held scanner. The image appears in a window of her workstation, as it appears on those of the others. (Others indicate that it has arrived and comment on it: "Oh yeah ... " "Not bad ... " "They're certainly after the same angle we are." "But it really is different than what Marty has done.") They proceed to discuss the competing ad and its similarities and differences from the current concept.

Scene shifts back to the creative director. At this point, he is visibly anxious to get this decision resolved. "I think this is it." The proposed single ad image appears on his workstation screen again. A suggestion comes from the binaural audio; it is the brand manager speaking: "Especially when I see what Racor did, I think we might do better to half-size the ad. It would be cheaper and I think we'd get an even better effect— providing we can get a good placement in the magazine. Can you try that, Marty?" Marty half-sizes the ad on his screen for display on the others.

The brand manager comments, "OK, Marty, let's go with that one. Scan us your final copy when it's ready." Marty shows great relief.

Scenario 2: "Omniview"

A key to successful investment is solid analysis based on timely information. Not surprisingly, firms in the financial sector hire an army of librarians, researchers, and analysts to identify trends—by market, by product, by company, even by country—the combinations are endless. Ever more of the desired information is available electronically, yet difficult access can make the information effectively unavailable at the moments when analysts and traders need it most.

This scenario describes an analyst's workstation providing access to information on demand from an ever-growing electronic data pool. The workstation offers access to distributed data, distributed processing, browsing, shared information space, and multimedia features, including audio (voice) and still video.

> The scene is a large investment banking firm. A discussion is under way: An analyst and a manager are talking over a research problem. A market specialist (a vice president) wants to make a major placement in a biotech start-up developing genetically altered seeds for agriculture. The bottom line to the biotech analyst: Will the investment fly? Manager to analyst: "This guy is hot to roll, so we need a report on the table for the investment committee by 9:00 A.M. tomorrow."

> The analyst is talking to himself: "Darn. I knew I should have begun looking at agribusiness last week." The analyst starts opening windows, displaying a menu of the databases available to him, both internal (for example, a "library" of all research reports written by his department) and external (Dow Jones, Lexis, Nexis, Dialog, and even video clips from network TV captured automatically by a remote server).

> He begins with a search for references to the company name, "BioAg." Selecting "new search" from a menu, he types the company name in a dialog box, specifies search perimeters (for example, how far back to look), then selects from a menu of databases. His choices: Nexis, Dow Jones, AP Wire, and Dialog. The system automatically dials into the various accounts simultaneously, using network bandwidth. As request results come in, they appear in a window.

> The analyst begins scanning information, assembling bits and pieces into different categories he's defined (or this

could be done automatically via agents). These categories will be the framework for his report: company market target, background (including management histories and investor profiles), overall market assessment, potential competitors, and possible partners. A window-based hypermedia structure facilitates this process: The analyst barely needs to type; almost everything is done by clicking and pointing. A nice extra: The system keeps a record of the discovery process that can be replayed backward or forward at high speed.

As he reads, the analyst is also defining new searches on the fly. A reference in one "hit" on the company name identifies two senior officers: The analyst posts searches for both, which run in the background as he goes back to reading the mailbox. Soon, a rhythm of inbound messages to the mailbox and outbound requests is set up.

Developing a market sector forecast is tricky. The analyst sends an "agent"—a special program able to identify promising information by use of context and content recognition techniques—off through the library of internal research files. It quickly identifies pieces of several reports offering forecasts of key department sectors such as U.S. agriculture, government support policy, and futures trading activity in potatoes and tobacco—two markets the analyst learned BioAg has targeted.

The report is fleshing out nicely. At this stage, the analyst is beginning to plow back through the data he has captured in each section, moving pieces and writing in commentary. The system automatically creates a "table of authorities" pointing to the sources of each piece of data.

Everything looks good, and the research has narrowed the issues down to one make-or-break question. The information collected so far leads the analyst to conclude the company will probably not fail in any case, but whether it will be a hit depends entirely on the success of one product—a low tar, low nicotine tobacco plant. In the past, with a deadline closing, the analyst would have scribbled in his best guess, but the system is easy to use, so he forges on.

The analyst mutters to himself, "Well, it boils down to two questions: How low in harmful qualities can they make the plants and still keep the taste, and what is going to happen in terms of tobacco regulation generally?" He sends off two agents to track down leads.

The agent searching the industry regulation trends returns with a reference to the TV show "60 Minutes," and the analyst notes it did a segment on tobacco firm liability some months before. He requests the clip, which is downloaded electronically. Viewing the clip, his thoughts crystallize. Noting the large sums the companies are spending to kill the suits, he blurts out, "Gosh! These guys are really scared—if BioAg can deliver, it will be their salvation." He tracks down additional information from Lexis, a legal/regulatory database, to back up his forecast, and wraps up the report.

The final scene is of the analyst hitting the "print" button and the report emerging from the printer. Simultaneously, he sends a copy electronically to his manager. The system will allow the manager not only to attach his notes to the report but also to look at the underlying data with ease. Close with phone conversation between the two. Analyst: "Yeah, the result is a surprise to me. I thought it was a turkey, but the data really support the investment. Look at it tonight—if you have any last minute changes, I can whip 'em out in the morning."

References

1. For a description of ISDN, see Chapter 10, "ISDN and Groupware."

12

Justifying Groupware

Measuring Productivity

Justifying groupware during the early exploration stages, when the focus is on one or a small number of teams, is quite different than when organizationwide implementation is the goal. In the early stages, justification must be geared toward the individual teams that are the first prospective users, with a focus on their incentives and constraints. Evaluation during these early stages must assess whether groupware helps a team do its job well and on time. Only then is groupware cost-justifiable.

A basic problem when justifying groupware is that most organizations do not have established criteria for measuring group productivity as it currently exists, let alone for what might happen if groupware is introduced. Current methods for group work are so accepted that they are not subject to scrutiny. Thus there is the real potential of rejecting groupware based on criteria that current systems couldn't pass. It is important that the introduction of groupware carry with it some accurate and accepted ways of thinking about and measuring group productivity.

If groupware has proven successful for individual business teams, it is possible to consider installation at the organizational level. This step often can require a major commitment of resources and can be difficult to justify to top management. It is often difficult to translate a successful single team application of groupware into a successful organizational application (one used by many different teams), so it is a good idea to begin by focusing on the tractable results of a small number of business teams.

There has been limited field experience with justifying groupware. One of the most impressive efforts we have seen is that done by IBM in its internal testing of the Decision Conference Center.[1] At IBM, the cost justification case was built during a series of pilot tests with real teams working on real problems. Pre- and post-questionnaires, interviews with users and managers, and use statistics gathered by the system were employed to track impacts of groupware use on variables such as

- time required for completing the project,
- number of meetings required,
- length of individual meetings,
- number of people in each group meeting, and
- cost (measured by time) of each team member.

Such measurements produce profiles of individual business teams. It is possible to determine whether goals were accomplished on time and to break down individual activities involved. It is also possible to position the team members as "early explorers" of the new technology of groupware who are being sent out to the "frontier." Part of their responsibility is to assess impacts not only on their own team, but on the company at large (if the groupware concept were to be extended beyond the pilot stage).

A second example comes from a major financial-services company that implemented a group-oriented data interpretation system (DIS)—a tool to give business users easy-to-use services for analyzing and communicating data within their group. At the end of the year-long pilot, the team members and system implementers requested that DIS be installed on a corporatewide basis for use by groups everywhere in the company. The cost was projected to be in the millions. The team reported few "hard-dollar" benefits, but the following "soft-dollar" benefits were enough for management to fund its request.

For end users, DIS benefits included clean-up and development of the business portfolio and an associated reduction in losses from bad accounts, an ability to price products more appropriately to local markets, enhanced communications between corporate offices and field sales, improved cross-functional teamwork, and improved competitive image. Although some of these sound like they could become hard-dollar benefits, no one was willing to attribute improvements just to the system—managers gave credit first to people and second to their ability to use tools innovatively to access data to improve the business.

For the system developers, DIS benefits included reduced development, optimizing, and debugging time; fewer phone calls from users for support; and increased developer satisfaction. Their rationale for wider implementation was that DIS encourages a team approach to development and promotes collaboration with users during development. For both end users and system developers, DIS was projected to create a cross-functional, cross-level, and cross-location coordination.

Although justification of groupware is just beginning, it is certainly possible to learn from efforts with other technologies, such as office automation and teleconferencing.[2] We have conducted justification efforts with other emerging technologies and have reviewed various research approaches. A basic checklist for the associated costs is provided in the "Checklist of Groupware Costs." Our goal in this checklist was to identify all the possible costs of ownership for the range of groupware options. Some of these options, of course, will be add-ons to existing infrastructure and thus will involve only incremental costs; others will require new infrastructure. Costs, of course, will vary greatly across different forms of groupware.

Benefits of Groupware

Looking at the benefits side of justification, here are the basic types of benefits that can be anticipated from groupware use.

Cost Reduction

The focus here is on cost efficiency: What costs can be reduced through the use of groupware? Examples might include reduction of the following: meeting time, time needed to complete a project, number of mistakes in which the "right" people were not present

Checklist of Groupware Costs

Initial System Costs

- Hardware
- Other equipment (tables, desks, etc.)
- Software (development, license, or rental charge)
- Warranty and/or maintenance contract
- Training
- Installation and set-up assistance

Staffing

- Groupware facilitators
- System manager/administrator(s)
- End-user support
- Programmers and analysts
- Operators
- Network personnel

System Growth and Maintenance

- Installation of engineering change orders
- Installation of new software
- Upgrades/new releases
- Documentation subscription services
- Network reconfiguration
- Ongoing/advanced training

at a meeting, rework where decisions were made and then questioned (by people who felt they should have been included), and production expenses because tools and output were shared by all team members.[3] Cost reduction concentrates on displacement or elimination of current business expenses through the use of groupware. *Same-time/same-place* groupware is the most straightforward to assess by such criteria, because the costs of meetings are quite visible and tractable—as are the improvements that groupware might offer.

Value-Added Benefits

Groupware has the potential to "add value" to business operations.[4] For example, groupware might improve the quality of decisions that are made by a team, new communication could occur via groupware that would not have occurred previously, faster and better responses to emergencies could become possible, or managerial control could be increased. Value-added benefits move beyond cost reduction; the most important benefits are aimed at effectiveness rather than efficiency. Value-added benefits are often more attractive but also more difficult to measure and connect directly to impacts of groupware—as opposed to other factors, such as effective leadership style.[5]

Unconventional Impacts

Groupware has the potential to alter how a team—and even an organization—works.[6] Groupware can yield unconventional impacts, many of which will be unpredictable. Examples of unconventional impacts are difficult to imagine but could include improvements like allowing new organizational units to develop which could not have grown through conventional media, encouraging group creativity and consideration of radical alternatives that might not otherwise have been identified or considered, or easing the pains of matrix management by providing a forum to resolve cross-organizational conflicts. It may require an intuitive leap for managers to move ahead with groupware on the basis of the prospect of unconventional benefits. Such benefits, of course, may be even more difficult to measure than value-added benefits, and they may be even more difficult to attribute to groupware—should they occur. Still, it is these surprise benefits of groupware that are likely to prove most important in the long run.

Introducing Groupware in a Large Organization

Justification of groupware should take account of all three classes of potential benefits noted above: cost reduction, value-added benefits, and unconventional impacts. As a general rule of thumb, a person leading the introduction of groupware in a large organization should consider the following five-step process:

1. Brainstorm about which benefits would most likely be achieved and be most convincing if they were achieved—given the type of groupware you are considering, the sorts of teams you will be working with, and what type of cost justification is necessary to meet your management's expectations.

2. Identify specific prospective users, concentrating on teams (and leaders) that will be good models for others to follow. The early users should not be people who "try anything" but, on the other hand, you probably don't want to start with your toughest case either. Work specifically with these early users to identify relevant cost/benefit measures to track. Be sure they are open to you tracking results for use in later cost-justification efforts for the organization at large.

3. Review successful justifications within your company for similar technologies, accepted by the same managers you must convince to pursue groupware. Look for evaluation variables at a similar level of specificity. Remember that justification is not a rigid science with prepackaged rules everyone accepts.

4. Conduct a series of early pilots, with careful evaluation of impacts. If you do not have time (say, six to nine months) for such pilots, look for and "enroll" believable early users who can give judgments regarding possible impacts on the company at large.

5. Do your final justification after the initial pilot results are in. The transition from pilot to ongoing use is critical and must be borne by some organization outside the team of users. The team will have met its needs when its job is done; they typically have little incentive to make groupware available to other parts of the company.

Justification has research, financial, and organizational change components. The research component means identifying variables linked to the productivity improvements you expect, and developing means for data collection and analysis.[7] The financial and organizational change components mean that you have to give management whatever they think they need to make a "go" or "no go" decision.

References

1. J. Nunamaker, D. Vogel, A. Heminger, B. Martz, R. Grohowski, and C. McGoff. "Experiences at IBM with group support systems: A field study." *Decision Support Systems* 5 (1989):183–196.

2. J. Charles. "Approaches to teleconferencing justification: Towards a general model." *Telecommunications Policy* 12(1981):296–303.

3. J. Nunamaker, D. Vogel, A. Heminger, B. Martz, R. Grohowski and C. McGoff. "Experiences at IBM with group support systems: A field study." *Decision Support Systems* 5(1989):183–196.

4. N. D. Meyer and M. E. Boone. *The Information Edge.* New York: McGraw-Hill Book Company, 1987.

5. F. Blackler and C. Brown. "Evaluation and the impact of information technologies on people in organizations." *Human Relations* 38(March 1985)3, 213–231.

6. R. Merrills. "How Northern Telecom competes on time." *Harvard Business Review* (July–August 1989):108–144.

7. P. Gray, D. Vogel, and R. Beauclair. "Assessing GDSS empirical research." *European Journal of Operations Research* (Spring 1990). See also A. Pinsonneault and K. L. Kraemer. "The impact of technological support on groups: An assessment of the empirical research." *Decision Support Systems* 5(1989):197–216.

13

Groupware Pitfalls

From Zealotry to Groupthink

When companies organize their workers in business teams and offer groupware to support them, the focus is often on the benefits of the new ways of working. What companies fail to focus on and anticipate, however, are the possible pitfalls of reorganizing the office. Without taking away from the great results that can come from using groupware, it is important to consider what can go wrong when business teams, armed with groupware, are turned loose.

We have divided our observations into two types of pitfalls: those that emerge from business teams and those that emerge from groupware.

Business Team Pitfalls

"Let's Do It Now" Zealotry

Task forces and business teams often are formed in the name of obtaining results faster than could be achieved in a conventional organization. The urgency of their business puts pressure on teams that typically results in a sense of compressed time, with little patience for delays. A team in such a state of time compression is more likely to grasp prematurely at answers and results that ignore either organizational or team needs. In the heat of a deadline, team goals may get far off track from the larger organization's needs. A team may make poor decisions by jumping without weighing alternatives sufficiently. Also, workers whose style is slower and more pensive may not be able to contribute effectively. The "let's do it now" mandate thus can be misdirected to lead a team down the wrong path with increasing speed.

The Bureaucratic Bypass Syndrome

Business teams offer a way to get things done without going through the normal protocols of large organizations. Such a bureaucratic bypass is appealing and invigorating. But there are dangers as well, if bypassing becomes a way of life and results in a rejection of the corporate structures that provide glue for the overall enterprise. A team that regularly bypasses corporate procedures may alienate other workers, who are more constrained by the norms of the organization; eventually, the remaining "bureaucrats" will find ways to put up roadblocks. What may be a win in the eyes of the team is likely to be perceived by the organization as a loss.

Entrepreneur's Disease

Business teams can be intoxicating in the same way that start-up ventures are. Such intoxication is very exciting and can contribute greatly to the success of the team. But some form of intoxication abuse can also creep into the picture. Business team members who become driven by the thrill of team performance may not make sound business decisions from the point of view of the larger organization. If the organization is not as responsive as the budding internal entrepreneurs would like, they may opt for a continuous fix of the bureaucratic bypass.

"I'm sorry I don't have that report for you . . .
Between answering E-mail, voice mail, and real
mail I don't have any time to get any work done."

Team Spirit Becomes Team Obsession

Teams often engender great loyalties. Teams provide immediate personal feedback and, typically, a strong sense of belonging and satisfaction. In contrast, the large corporations or government agencies within which business teams work may seem cool and impersonal. Business teams also can compete with personal commitments. Teams often prompt the kind of personal involvement typical of political campaigns, or even wars. An individual's loyalty and identification with the team may be stronger than that with the company. Family life also may take a back seat to the work of the team. Team leaders must work hard to strike an appropriate balance in this subtle—but critical—aspect of team life.

Too Little, Too Late

Management must make a clear statement of the work team's importance—and back it up with a clear commitment of resources. If workers are assigned to teams without having relief from other duties, they may become overloaded. The work of the team as well as other work may suffer. Managers of other projects will think twice about cannibalizing their own projects by committing people and other resources to a project for which they don't have responsibility. Moreover, if a team is given a responsibility without being given sufficient authority to allocate resources and make decisions, it will not be able to function effectively.

Team Rewards

Existing compensation structures in most organizations are oriented toward rewarding the performance of individuals. Incentives for performing as a team are not yet well established. Reward structures that favor individual performance may interfere with effective team performance.

Groupware Pitfalls

Overselling Groupware

It is the kiss of death for a technology to be branded the important technology of the year. Groupware has received that kind of attention. People who are responsible for implementing groupware must beware of taking their own hype too seriously. It is important not to overpromise to users. The most likely place that overpromising might occur is in the area of integration. In the short run, groupware solutions are not likely to be integrated with other important tools. The state of the art is just not that advanced, and there are many infrastructure and logistics hurdles to clear before groupware tools are gracefully integrated with other tools. In fact, the best way to avoid the overselling pitfall may be not to sell the concept of groupware at all, but rather to view it as an extension to applications and technologies people already are using. It should also be made clear that groupware cannot overcome organizational inefficiencies; it cannot change how a company does business unless the company is willing to change itself.

"Do It My Way—Or Else"

Some forms of groupware, including commitment management, group decision support, and project management, lend themselves to abuse by a strong group leader. These tools impose a structure on how the group does its work—an analytic framework for a group decision, or a planning approach for project management. The group leader, by controlling how these tools are used, can exert an unreasonably high degree of control over how the group operates. This tends to make work on the team unpleasant for other participants, as well as interfere with the effectiveness of the team by limiting diversity of work styles and approaches. The line between charisma and autocracy may be a fine one.

"Do It the Software's Way—Or Else"

Certain software approaches to groupware build in a strong set of preconceptions about how the work of a group should get done. A conversational structuring program, for example, that forces all communications into a set philosophy may be too rigid for some teams. If the software doesn't fit or adapt itself to the needs and style of the group, the members are unlikely to use it over time.

Groupthink

Some groupware that supports the work of face-to-face meetings may sacrifice the benefits of individual creativity in favor of the creativity of the group. Tools that are used for group brainstorming will favor those people who are quick thinkers and who produce well in a somewhat pressured group setting. Other people may prefer to do their creative work away from the group and have the group react to and improve on that work. Groupware and team leaders must accommodate both styles.

Uncoordinated Groupware

Many groupware systems can be installed and used by small groups of workers—an organizationwide commitment is not necessary for effective groupware use. If different parts of an organization adopt different groupware applications, environments, and platforms, then there will be difficulty in coordinating the work of different teams in the organization. Individuals who work on several teams will be faced with the problem of working in incompatible environments. Groupware standards are a long way off—until then, there will remain a measure of duplication of effort and difficulty reconciling incompatible groupware systems.

In Conclusion

Notice that most of these pitfalls are distortions of a good thing, rather than a simple evil. The list is not intended to be inclusive; it is intended to be provocative. You, as groupware practitioners, will want to develop your own list; your organizational context will determine which pitfalls you need to take most seriously. The important point is to remember that groupware pitfalls are real and have the potential to blindside even the most careful implementation plan. By considering such pitfalls in advance, the downsides of groupware are avoidable.

Part III
Turning Groups into Teams

14

Putting Technology Before the Horse

*Technology Matters, but Team
Dynamics Matter More*

The word "groupware" makes most people wince. It sounds too much like a software program or a fancy technology. Groupware certainly encompasses these things; but above all, groupware is an *approach* to using our new technological tools to satisfy an organizational need—the support of business teams. This larger goal is not something organizations can realize overnight. Even companies with a long history of supporting and sustaining teams are experiencing new challenges in a changing competitive environment. Viewing groupware as a technology can lead to a

"quick fix" attitude—"All our problems will be solved once we install this package." Technology never works that way. Simple technological fixes generally end up being neither a fix, nor simple.

The problem is that we become transfixed by our new technologies, and too often we end up putting the technology cart before the organizational horse. The best way to implement groupware is to develop a conceptual framework tailored to specific corporate objectives before ever buying the first software package or installing the first LAN. This framework need not be complicated, but it should encompass the strategic goals to be realized and account for the individual needs of employees.

We believe in experimenting with new technologies early. Computers, software, and communications are changing so rapidly that it is impossible for a company to stay on the leading edge by taking the usual think/plan/implement approach. This philosophy of aggressive experimentation sounds antithetical to the attitude of working within a framework, but it really is not.

We believe that the successful companies will be the ones who adopt early, experiment aggressively, and don't hesitate to toss expensive purchases into the dumpster if they turn out to fit poorly with their objectives. This is where the framework comes in—users should test new technologies against the artificial horizon of strategic goals as an antidote to credulous acceptance of glittering new technologies.

At the extreme, the best way to keep the horse in front of the cart is to go to the limits of aggressive experimentation. Consider experimenting with a technology that you are already certain you will not roll out within your organization. For example, the "executive information systems" available today often fall short of delivering what executives really need. A decision to install such a system companywide at this point would be dubious at best—it might not meet real business needs, and it could lock a company into an old technology just when breakthroughs are about to occur. On the other hand, limited experimentation with such a system (say, within a workgroup) could yield insights about what to expect from more advanced systems to come—especially the organizational impacts of using such a system.

This is where the willingness to dispose of expensive technology becomes so important. A test system might be an utter failure operationally, but it might still amount to a tremendous success because of the organizational learnings it offers. The problem is that most company's reward structures are not set up in a way that rewards employees for such successes— the employee who brings in a winning executive information system will get the kudos, but the individual who recommends a system that never rolls out will get very little attention indeed. The net effect more often puts technology before the horse as employees identify so closely with one form of "success" that they end up evangelizing for a technology that does not fit corporate needs.

Ultimately, the best way to keep technology in the proper perspective is to communicate strategic goals to every individual in the company. This in turn will greatly increase the chances that teams will ask themselves where their efforts fit within a larger corporate technological framework.

15

Anticipating Group Dynamics

Catching the Turns

Weather, water, economics, traffic, families, and teams are familiar, chaotic systems. In their dynamic states, they outstrip precise formulation. Their quieter states aren't what people want to know about. Historically, most scientists have preferred distinguishing finer and finer particles and have developed precise mathematics for dealing with nonchaotic phenomena, but family therapists, organizational consultants, meteorologists, biologists, and a growing group of cross-disciplinary chaos theorists are plunging into the problem of describing dynamic systems.

From this exchange a rapidly growing understanding of group process is emerging. Using action research tools, extensive direct experience, and a gut sense that people in relationship form the archetypal molecule for organizational systems, pioneers are roughing out the "rules" for this new territory. Many conclude that teams may be the central players in information-rich businesses of the future. In this chapter we explore some of these emerging ideas, show how they can be used to diagnose team dynamics, and, most importantly, identify the critical moments or "turns" a team can make as it moves from obstacle to action.

Converting Understanding into Tools

Members of our team have spent over 20 years as professional process consultants and facilitators, leading thousands of meetings, guiding countless groups through planning, problem solving, decision-making, and production processes. Lately, we've been fascinated with turning these experiences into tools that help others lead effective group process. This venture has taken us into the very challenging problem of articulating clearly what we think we know intuitively. How can people learn to "read the group" or recognize the "turns" in process? What should one look at or for? Will tools help?

Groupware as a class of tools embodies many implicit answers for understanding group dynamics, as discussed elsewhere in this book. Groupware also will eventually help with diagnostics. But any work with teams, as with any selection of groupware, starts with raising one's own awareness about what actually is going on, during times of both slow performance and heightened activity.

Two Beginning Choices: "Stop Action?" or "In Action?"

Looking at teams poses a dilemma right away. Do we look at a group in stop action so we can count parts and appreciate char-

acteristics? Or do we look at the group in process, as a dynamic phenomenon acting interdependently over time?

As facilitators, we greatly prefer looking at groups in process, since our explicit role is to guide people at the process level. Besides, groups seen in stop action are as different as any other collection of living things on Earth: They are factory floor teams that work on shifts; they are design teams that work on advanced workstations, often in great isolation; they are task forces that combine functional experts to solve integration programs; they are councils with loose formal relations; and they are management teams with precise relations. Families are groups. Scout troops are groups. The variety is endless.

On the other hand, seen as a process, groups share many similar properties. They all fluctuate in and out of being organized. They all are loose in the beginning before people know each other and anything's possible, and they get tight when critical decisions about people, time, and money have to be made. All groups have to settle on some specific way of working that everyone can commit to. It doesn't matter what the approach is; it must be shared, or group members won't be able to integrate activities. And all groups must master these commitments to some degree to experience anything like high performance. These things are true regardless of what the group looks like.

We have known for a long time that process is similar across many different settings, and we were recently very excited to read in James Gleick's book *Chaos*[1] that scientists are finding dynamic systems the world over which share this characteristic. It shows up most dramatically in fractal studies, where patterns of complexity repeat no matter what level of magnification is used. This phenomenon, called "scaling," rises from the fact that the visible patterns of a fractal display are generated by relatively simple dynamic elements that play out similarly throughout itself—at both the macro and micro levels.

Strange Attractors: Patterns that Connect

While being formed, patterns like those found in cloud formations or water turbulence are unpredictable in detail, moment to moment; but when looked at over time, by processing thousands of variables graphically on a computer, the process itself falls into patterns with boundaries. Chaos scientists call these patterns "strange attractors"—a kind of process order in chaos. They have found that in fact there is no such state as complete randomness. There are always seeds of order.

We think the same "attractors" work with teams as dynamic systems. After years of graphically recording team processes on large charts and looking at dynamics over time, we have come to see some of these patterns. They don't work predictably and in a precise way—but they are central in guiding awareness by suggesting what to look for and suggesting patterns that often play out in practice. Such distinctions—or characteristics of group behavior—will most surely provide the specifications for any groupware that actually achieves widespread usefulness in the years to come.

Process Models

A sample of such a pattern is one we learned from Will Schutz,[2] an early pioneer in group dynamics. He claims that all group members go through a three-stage psychodynamic process to meet basic needs when they enter into face-to-face relationships. These needs are:

1. inclusion ("Am I a part of this group?"),

2. control ("What will be my role and status?"), and

3. affection ("Will I get the emotional satisfaction I want from this group?")

Schutz has built a whole test called the FIRO-B around this assumption; he uses it as a key tool for group diagnostics. He holds that people go through this pattern every time they return from a break or lunch hour. One can begin observing a group in terms of this pattern and see many familiar dynamics come to light. For instance, think about any group you know that has had members who know each other well and then had a new member join. The old members are sharing affection. The new member is concerned about inclusion. Critical turbulences begin and can be disruptive if none of the old members realizes that spending a little time including the new person is important.

Allan Drexler worked with Jack Gibb and Marvin Weisbord in the 1960s to develop a handy four-step, team-building model.[3] It states that all groups need to handle the following four concerns (in order):

1. "Why am I here?"
2. "Who are you (and what will you ask of me)?"
3. "What are we doing?" and
4. "How will we do it?"

Bruce Tuckman has yet another model.[4] It breaks team building into four stages. These stages are

1. forming (a group gets together, settles membership),
2. storming (struggles for control and roles),
3. norming (makes clear agreements and goals), and
4. performing (does the work).

Thinking like a musician listening for harmonies, one can detect a rough parallel between the Schutz, Drexler, and Tuckman models. Although the perspective is different, the needs, concerns, and stages are similar. The pattern in common is a movement from open possibility or freedom, to constraint, and then to performance. These patterns repeat, and keep repeating for any group.

Describing Turns

A feature of this freedom-to-constraint-to-freedom cycle is the fact that it happens in fits and starts. Dynamic systems, especially in times of chaos, change suddenly. Periods of evolution are followed by crisis. Larry Griener at Harvard looks at the overall development of organizations from this perspective. Whatever is being done at the moment is a choice to neglect other things. They build up and demand attention. Crisis happens, and another period of evolution occurs. For instance, an entrepreneur builds up a great amount of potential in a business, but creates a crisis in direction. Not everything can be done. The way out is a period of leadership, often by someone with more operating expertise capable of sustaining a consistent momentum. This results in good people joining up but precipitates a crisis of autonomy. The new people want running room. So this leads to a period of decentralization, etc.

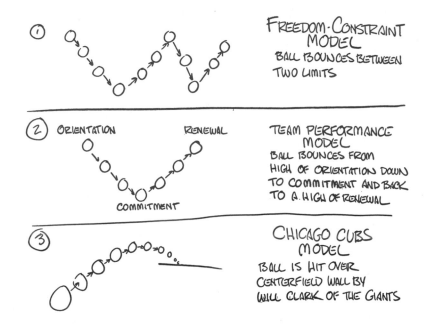

Using a Ball to Show a Framework

At a team level, this same kind of fluctuation occurs, but is seldom reflected in models of team process. The Team Performance Model (Fig. 2.5) shows this crisis as a 90° turn. It happens when a process converges to a point of constraint and must turn dramatically in order to regain flexibility and momentum. Within the model each stage is, in fact, a mini-process with a turn of this sort. Understanding these turns begins to create a critical moments diagnostic tool.

The purpose of this chapter is not to explain these models but to show how they are critical in diagnosing team dynamics and are representative of a kind of nonelectronic groupware. In addition, these models serve to make team members themselves aware of their own styles and patterns of working together.

The Key Is Making Process Visible

To see what is happening in a dynamic system you literally have to use some kind of tool that lets you map the process over time. By definition, this would have to be something that can record thousands of data points and facilitate comparison in meaningful ways. To be useful in action, it would have to be a tool that could be remembered in one's head.

This sounds more difficult than it is. In the first place, our brains are quite used to doing this. We take in multi-sensory information at incredible rates, and we map it into general understandings we have of how the world works. These are often called mental models, or world views. We think of them as the biological equivalent of computer operating systems. Our attention does not often deal with raw data, but rather with the waves of understanding we experience as data matches model. Only in breakdown do we look at things as they are—it's confusing and chaotic—and if one is not aware of the interdependence of chaos and order, things look very disturbing. But new order is always just around the corner. It's when we are in the dark that we most need the abstract tools as distinguished from our heavily elaborated models drawn from real experience. They become means of getting above the chaos to see the coming order.

One client organization calls this kind of thinking "helicoptering." Let's take a ride and see what shows up.

Levels of Team Functioning

The first thing we see is constant motion and cycling. Teams fluctuate between periods of order and clarity (constraint) and between periods of uncertainty (freedom). We see this clearly in sports teams. Winning streaks are not permanent—nor are low

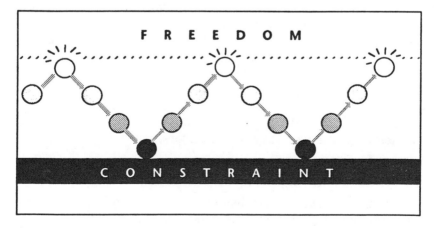

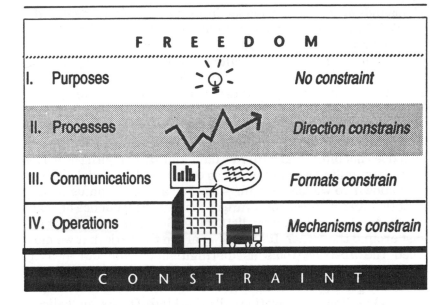

Figure 15.1

periods. The team improves or dissolves; players are traded. The same happens in business. Cycles are inherent; their period and length are unpredictable, but their existence is a given.

Helicoptering over organizations, we can see that the levels of function differ in how dynamic they are, partly due to the constraints at each level. (See Fig. 15.1.)

When we look at operations, some aspects of group dynamics move so slowly we are apt to think of them as objects, or physical constants. These are the constants of work, and they compose the structures and mechanisms through which we get things done. These can be touched, photographed, and counted. But breakdowns do occur at this level, and when they do they are compelling and demand action. In general, Abraham Maslow was correct in saying that, when survival issues (read "operational issues") are at stake, they take number-one priority.[5]

Looking at Communications

Group communications are dynamic, because no system of symbols can totally constrain how people feel about information they are encountering—meaning is always inexact. To see communications dynamics, some record must be made that allows for a comparison of patterns. These various ways we record communications also determine to a great extent what we pay attention to.

David Sibbet has worked for years recording what groups say, using large wall displays. He creates a literal "group memory" around the room. Not only does he see what's being communicated, but so does everyone else. The points of convergence and divergence show up graphically. If David creates a timeline display that uses consistent symbols, with circles for meetings (sized large and small to correspond to the number of people attending), the group can see many things at a glance. Meetings are used to mark key turns in process, such as announcing new goals, celebrating endings, or dealing with alignment. Bunched-up circles indicate an intense period. Spaced out circles would indicate a well-operating team or a weakening of commitment. No observation in isolation informs, but together with other insights, it can be a key diagnostic insight.

Formal inventories are also a tried and true way of assessing team communication issues and other dynamic problems. The consistency of the inventory used throughout an organization provides a mirror that eventually becomes a very sensitive diagnostic tool. Computers that can compare various inventory results can provide a graphic depiction of norms.

Correspondence files are another mirror for process at the communications level. Electronic mail provides the potential for even more insight if methods of displaying messages improve. (Currently the small screen and linear quality obscure much of the process information, but memory and search functions will reveal it.)

This issue of looking at frameworks is itself a source of critical moments for teams. When teams have conflicting ways of organizing information or translating communications, confusion develops quickly. This problem increases with geographic separation and cultural differences. Some kind of consistency is required for any communication to work. When a team finds a model or metaphor or clear action plan that everyone understands, this is often the turn within implementation processes. When this breaks down because a new manager doesn't understand a prior way of looking at things, then turmoil results.

Since groupware must inherently make assumptions about how people structure communications, any people lying outside those assumptions will be quite resistant to the tools.

Looking at Processes

A much more dynamic level of group life is the emotional and energetic phenomenon revealed in group process. Humans are 80% water; everything about us is always in motion. We are incredible sensors of our environment. In meetings we literally smell each other, though it's not the norm to talk about it. We sense shifting in seats, hear group indications of approval and rejection in mutterings and sighs. Body language, voice tone, sequence, and pace of conversation are all monitors of the energy levels.

Charts and graphics provide a clue to this domain if they are hand-generated. The line quality of markers and the movement embodied in drawings are tracks of our energetic field. Handwriting experts can tell much about a person. A skilled facilitator, orchestrating groups through collective drawing activity, can tell just as much. (Maintaining the richness of this visual information is a central challenge of input/output for groupware tools as we become more computerized.)

But most of the time these energetic dynamics are "read" by directly feeling the group in action. With emotion, the direction is all important. Are people moving toward or away from commitment? Are things getting more or less tense? Is conflict increasing or decreasing?

Video feedback tools provide a good way for people to see themselves in a team context; they increasingly are used to train people to be aware of this level of process. The most critical moments occur when these energies are blocked or thwarted. They go somewhere, usually bottling up and creating high pressure, even explosive conditions. They also have a tendency to show up in other kinds of areas. If key people on a team have a bad relationship but are consciously unaware of it or don't want to confront it, they may unconsciously subvert the work of the team so that they don't have to deal with the issue.

These second-level, hidden agenda issues cannot be diagnosed directly, but they can be looked for in interviews and private conversations or flushed out by inventories. Ways of bringing this information back to the team is part of the art of team building and organizational development. Within the many ways, the key objective is to provide the feedback in a way that group members see its validity.

Looking at Consciousness

There is a level of group process neither bounded by time, nor directly observable; yet it is one of the most critical dimensions, particularly in long-term high performance. This is the level of the group consciousness or group spirit.

We are all light-processing beings. We can have visions and imagine nonexistent things. In our inner minds we collapse time, hop through space, and perform amazing feats of insight. Modern physicists like David Bohm claim that humans share an "implicate order" with the universe and that we are, in a very literal sense, all manifestations of the whole. This aspect of groups must be assumed. Analysis does not yield this information—it can't be charted—but it makes all the difference.

For years we have led top management teams in planning processes. We analyze the business environment, conclude about the industry and competitors, identify strengths and opportunities, and commit to key objectives. These processes all feel like a journey into constraint (and sometimes hell). As optimistic and open as everyone is at the beginning, by commitment time the issues are heavy and the stakes high. No one feels very free at this point. Will the group coalesce? At these points the group is, in fact, in crisis. If there is no movement forward, confidence can wane; momentum will be lost. This turning point isn't hard to detect. The team facilitator, the team members, everyone will feel it. Things are "stalled out."

Yet at this very moment, again and again, somebody is able to see a way that furthers the game. It often feels like a spot of light or vision, which enters at the point of greatest risk. If, in fact, the group has laid a trustworthy base of shared information, if basic trust relationships are in place, and if the team is not destitute of resources when this idea enters the discussion, it is like a match in a dark room, or a door opening. The group turns.

Group leaders are those who can articulate these directions in the times of crisis. They may or may not hold the official reins. But they can "jump" the action. In good teams, the whole group "gets it" and turns. Sometimes only a critical nucleus can see the direction but is capable of leading the rest along. The addition of consciousness to all the other factors catalyzes these turns.

In Summary

Diagnosing team dynamics requires some kind of process framework that can be held with part of one's attention while one makes direct observations with the other parts of the mind. The framework serves as a map or mirror for the data and allows one to see patterns.

The most important pattern to look for is the cycling between freedom and constraint that happens at all levels of process. The turns occur when teams decide how to arrange the constraints so that some freedom re-enters the picture. These solutions work for a while but precipitate new constraints or crises. With practice, one can come to understand that breakdown and crises are actually integral to forward movement. A shift in the constraints allows new ideas and patterns to emerge.

Groupware that helps team members see their own process will help with raising everyone's awareness of these dynamics. Groupware that narrows the field of awareness to achieve efficiencies in one level—say, communications—will eventually develop problems in the neglected areas.

There seems to be no way out of this fluctuation. But it is possible to learn about it and use the dynamics to a team's advantage. This—like surfing or helicoptering—takes experience, of course. But wonderful increases in effectiveness take place by simply shifting to a process view now and then and seeing the interdependencies and connections that tie us all together in action.

References

1. J. Gleick. *Chaos: Making a New Science*. New York: Viking Penguin, Inc., 1987.

2. W. Schutz. *FIRO: A Three-Dimensional Theory of Interpersonal Behavior*. Muir Beach, Calif.: WSA, 1989. Original publication 1959.

3. A.B., Drexler, D. Sibbet, and R.H. Forrester. "The team performance model." *Team Building: Blueprints for Productivity*. W. B. Reddy and K. Jamison (eds.). San Diego, Calif.: National Training Laboratory, Institute for Behavioral Sciences, 1988:45–61; L.P. Bradford, J. R. Gibb, and K. D. Benne. *T-Group Theory and Laboratory Method: Innovation in Re-Education*. J. Wiley, 1967; M.R. Weisbord. *Organizational Diagnosis*. Reading, Mass.: Addison-Wesley Publishing Company, 1978 (1985 printing).

4. B.W. Tuckman. "Developmental sequence in small groups." *Psychological Bulletin* 63(1965):384–399.

5. A.H. Maslow. *Toward a Psychology of Being*. Princeton, N.J.: Van Nostrand, 1962.

16

What Is a Facilitator, Anyway?

Suggestions for Successful Meetings

Have you ever endured an overly-ambitious, never-ending meeting without even an agenda—let alone clear objectives—and wondered "Why me?" Such interminable, pointless meetings inspire some people to want to jump up and say, "I'll run this meeting!" Anyone so inclined is a potential facilitator.

A facilitator is someone who guides a meeting and helps make it work by using professional skills to draw out the best in

people. A facilitator trusts that people in the meeting will make the best decision and will know what to do next, given the right environment in which to do it. A facilitator's role is like that of a mountain guide preparing to take a group hiking. The guide assesses the group's needs by asking questions like, "Where are you going?" "How much hiking experience do you folks have?" and "What do you want to get out of this hike?"

Effective facilitators tend to take a long view of a meeting and see it in the context of the entire group or a particular project. Meetings are often the turning points in the life of a project, but it is people—and how they interact—that bring a project to life. This group dynamic is shared in meetings to align on roles, goals, information, and scheduling. A simple process map that identifies what happens before, during, and after a meeting is a useful way to approach a meeting. A process map shows the whole picture and sequences events so the facilitator can anticipate and coach the other people involved.

A key for success is to get involved early. Although facilitators get called in at various points in the meeting process, they have greater success when they are involved at the beginning.

Before the Meeting: Ask Good Questions, Then Listen!

The process of guiding a meeting begins with a genuine curiosity in discovering what it takes to get the group collaborating effectively. A needs assessment will help you determine how you can support this effort. The assessment should consider a range of questions including the following:

- *Who called the meeting and what is its overall purpose?* Obvious, perhaps, but a bit of time thinking through a meeting's purpose can help create a much more focused meeting or might uncover another way of reaching the group's goals (that is, the meeting may not be needed at this time).
- *Who are the meeting participants?* Help the person who called the meeting to sort out who should be invited and who should stay informed. Gather background information that will help you identify potential pitfalls, as well as opportunities for cooperation. Who is new to the team?

Who is likely to have "hidden agendas" that will surface and need to be addressed?

- *What level of meeting documentation is needed?* Documenting a meeting could involve one or more of the following:

  minutes to inform people who were not at the meeting about what happened when, who is responsible, and what the next steps will be;

  graphic recording during the meeting allowing the group to see what is happening as it unfolds and to increase participation;

  electronic meeting technology (for example, using an electronic whiteboard to record a mission statement, or using a computer to record a strategic plan) so participants can leave the meeting with documents in hand;

  a follow-up report to annotate the meeting process from a "bird's eye view"—including reductions of the graphic recording and handouts; and

  videotape to record key moments and show the group its process in action.

- *Is the meeting room ready?* Before the meeting, make sure the meeting room is available and arranged with the seating you need. Make sure all the equipment (copyboards, flip charts, projectors, video equipment, computers, and so on) and supplies are available to support this group. Just before the meeting is to begin, check out the equipment, make sure someone can operate it, and know where the extra supplies are (extra bulb for the projector, extra paper and markers for the electronic copyboard, etc.). Plan for food to sustain energy, and have the temperature adjusted on the cool side to keep everyone alert.

- *Invite or inform the meeting participants.* Give them adequate lead time to add the meeting to their schedule and prepare for it.

- *Plan and publish the agenda.* For any item, define the objectives, desired outcomes, topic "owner," and approximate time to reach closure. Consider what process you will use to achieve a realistic outcome within a reasonable time frame. If you have time, publish a draft agenda and request feedback—changes, additions, wordsmithing—from all or key participants. By giving participants a stake in developing the agenda, you can determine commitment or resistance and be prepared to handle it. At the very least, publish an agenda one or two days before the meeting with a statement of the meeting's purpose so everyone can come mentally prepared.

- *Assemble the meeting support team and get clarity on roles and responsibilities.* Roles may include those of facilitator, meeting manager, graphic or technical recorder, and people who provide technical support, to whom the facilitator may need to assign specific responsibilities for preparing meeting documentation.

During the Meeting: Be Flexible and Responsive to the Group

The facilitator's role during the meeting is to guide the group to its desired outcomes and create an atmosphere where everyone can safely contribute to the process. Getting agreements along the way helps the following steps go more smoothly.

- *Clarify roles with the group.* Explain the role of the facilitator, manager, and recorders and any related tools they will be using which are new to the group. Explaining your role can be an opportunity to model the level of disclosure you would like from the group.

- *Review the agenda and purpose.* This helps orient people to what is happening and what might be expected of them. Part of a facilitator's responsibility is to make people feel comfortable. Post the agenda and briefly review all the items at a general level, clarifying the objectives and desired outcomes and agreeing upon the time allotted for each item. Ask if other topics should be added, what their objectives and outcomes are, and how long they will take. Reprioritize the agenda, adding or deleting items.

- *Review or create with the group the ground rules* for participation, decision-making, and other processes you will be using, like brainstorming, prioritizing, and voting.

- *Introduce each agenda topic.* As you begin to work through each agenda item, have the topic owner state the objectives—for example, provide status information, brainstorm issues, or come to agreement. Also state the desired outcome (for example, understanding of status information with discussion of issues, prioritizing issues, or unanimous agreement). Describe the process you plan to use to reach closure and invite participants to ask questions until they understand what is expected of them. Ask someone to act as timekeeper and keep the group apprised of the allotted time remaining for each topic. If it's a four-hour discussion, state the time each hour; and perhaps 30 minutes before the end of the discussion ask if the remaining time is enough to meet the objective and desired outcome. If it's a 30-minute discussion, have the timekeeper indicate when 10 minutes are left. Time can thus be used to motivate the group to meet its objective for the agenda topic.

- *Remain invisible to the group.* Stay out of the content and focus on the process that will help the group find its way through the content issues. Monitor the meeting environment and the effects of the process on group members.

- *Take care to maintain the high energy of participants.* Plan for breaks at least every two hours. For meetings over a meal time, plan for whether you'll break to attend lunch outside or have an inside, working lunch.

- *Create a safe environment* where participants can be open and use their talents optimally.

- *Manage conflict,* and live through strategic moments in a group. Use simple techniques like restating what the group is experiencing, or focus the attention on the group memory (recorder's work on the wall). Be willing to change the agenda when things aren't going well.

- *Encourage commitment to action* by focusing on next steps, responsibilities, and target dates.

- *Evaluate the meeting.* Review what was completed and what is still outstanding. Create an Action List, and assign tasks if necessary. Ask the group to say what worked and what needs improvement in further meetings. Assess the process as well as the results. Draft an agenda for the next meeting, if it is part of an ongoing process.

After the Meeting: Follow Up as Promised—When You Said You Would!

- *Create and distribute the documentation* (annotated, if required).
- *Communicate next steps* with an Action List.
- *Review the meeting* with the group's manager or leader. Get feedback to improve the next meeting.
- *Incorporate agreed-upon improvements* from the group into the next meeting.

Numerous books and articles have been written on running productive meetings.[1] And groupware can help—either within a meeting or by reducing the number or length of meetings. But so, too, can improving the meeting process itself and using a good facilitator.

Meeting $ $ $

The financial impact of unproductive meetings is enormous. Let's say a large corporation has 1000 managers, each spending ten hours per week in meetings. These managers are paid $50 per hour ($500 per week times 1000 equals $500,000 per week for the time they spend in meetings). If 25% (a conservative estimate) of their meeting time is unproductive, the corporation is losing $125,000 per week on meeting inefficiency! Computed annually, that's about $6 million per year.

References

1. M. Doyle and D. Straus. *The Interaction Method: How to Make Meetings Work.* New York: Jove Books, 1976. See also R. K. Mosvick and R. B. Nelson. *We've Got to Start Meeting Like This.* Glenview, Ill.: Scott, Foresman Professional Publishing Group, 1987; and S. L. Tubbs. *A Systems Approach to Small Group Interaction.* Reading, Mass.: Addison-Wesley Publishing Company, 1984.

17

Sustainable Benefits Come from Training and Support

The Human Side of the Groupware Equation

Boring, you say? Maybe so, but we guarantee that if you don't pay attention to training and support, you will neither reap the benefits of groupware nor see any return on your investment. For evidence, in its widely read article, "The Puny Payoff from Office Computers,"[1] *Fortune* magazine documented that companies spent millions of dollars on word processors and personal computing, with minimal return on investment (see "Top Ten Reasons Why Office Automation Failed").

STUDY IN
INVINCIBLE
FORMS
OF
TECHNOLOGY

"Ya see, Captain, we didn't run into an iceberg . . . It's a huge pile of scrapped business computers."

Top Ten Reasons Why Office Automation (OA) Failed*

1. Met no real business need
2. Uncommitted management
3. Inadequate training and support
4. Poor internal marketing of OA (no education on the benefits)
5. Inadequate user participation in decisions affecting them
6. Insufficient planning
7. Inadequate system evaluation
8. System problems during pilot
9. Unskilled change agents
10. Poor project implementation management

Almost every reason for office automation's failure can be attributed to poor training and support. Here are some reasons why.

- *Office automation met no real business need.* Support should have included definition and mapping of needs to product functionality.
- *Inadequate training and support.* Software for office automation, spreadsheet, word processing, and database management software was given to users with minimal training on how to apply it, and poor support was provided when users got in trouble.
- *Poor internal marketing of OA.* Internal consultants, usually within information systems, did a poor job of educating management to the benefits and pitfalls of office automation.

---

* As selected and ranked by user and information systems managers in 80 *Fortune* 1000 companies in New York, Chicago, San Francisco, and Toronto in research sponsored by Alexia Martin in 1984.

- *Insufficient planning.* Another aspect of support that was lacking was a plan for technology implementation, configuration, and installation.
- *System problems during pilot.* Technical support from empathetic support personnel should have been mandatory during implementation of new technology.

And the list goes on and on. Let's not repeat mistakes when implementing groupware. Some groupware enthusiasts argue that groupware training and support is unnecessary because the new technology is transparently easy and natural to use. Not true. It is tempting but equally hazardous to omit training and support when groupware tools are just plugged into an existing business team that has a pressing need for performance aids. For example, a team of designers in the United States and engineers in Asia needs to discuss manufacturing issues weekly to make a seamless handoff from design to manufacturing. Trans-Pacific travel for this two-hour meeting is out of the question. A video teleconference meeting allowing the designers and engineers to see each other along with their drawings and models is one solution. But someone must know how to initiate and run the video teleconference session so that all participants can benefit from best use of the medium.

We see an evolution of tools occurring from stand-alone "personal productivity" end user computing applications, to "workgroup" productivity tools, and finally, to a *connected* workgroup phase. This third phase requires an architected view of information and technology—an infrastructure providing access to integrated groupware applications as well as to local and corporate data through flexible communications and advanced technology.

If organizationwide benefits are to accrue from connected workgroups, training and support must become key infrastructure issues. At another manufacturing company where video teleconferencing was implemented for a multisite engineering team, it started to die when the engineers needed to communicate with other workgroups who had no access to the tools. It died completely at the end of the project, because an organizational infrastructure was not in place to provide training or ongoing support for extended use.

Definition of Training and Support

Training is instruction on *how* to use groupware. As such, it is specific to the tools and methodologies involved. We distinguish training from education, which involves *why* to use groupware and what the benefits and pitfalls of groupware are. Both are important.

Support is everything it takes to get users up and running with groupware tools. It is also everything it takes to help users continue to meet their objectives.

Some training and support is easy and need not be pervasive. If the groupware is location-specific, such as in a meeting room, meeting facilitators or team leaders who use the location need to be trained (see Table 17.1). Support can be handled by local personnel—secretarial/administrative support, local information and telecommunications services, or even facilities services, the folks who often already provide meeting support (see Table 17.2).

Other types of groupware are network and communication based. These types of groupware require more extensive training and support to enable people to communicate effectively beyond the walls of their team. Of course, you may start by training just the group's members supported by a local area network, but experience shows that they soon want to expand their connections with others; and as connected workgroups become the norm more people need support and training. This *any-time/any-place* groupware demands extensive training and support. (See Fig. 17.1.)

Initial and Ongoing Training and Support

To get started, team leaders and/or members need some training to acclimate to groupware, its benefits, and its technical uses. Managers, particularly, need to understand the benefits and pitfalls of groupware. Ongoing training is needed to keep users constantly adapting groupware—"teach a man to fish and he never goes hungry." None of this training need be delivered through traditional classroom-based training. Manuals, "cheat

Table 17.1
Primary and Secondary Groupware Support Providers

Groupware	Corporate Information Systems/Telcom	Local Information Systems/Telcom	Administrative Support	Professional Meeting Facilitator or Leader
Same-time / Same place				
· Electronic copyboard		Secondary	Primary	
· PC projectors	Secondary	Primary		
· Group decision rooms	Secondary	Primary		
· Polling systems	Secondary	Primary		Secondary
Same-time / Different-place				
· Conference calls		Secondary	Primary	
· Screen sharing	Secondary	Primary		
· Video teleconferencing	Secondary	Primary		
Different-time / Same-place				
· Team rooms	Secondary	Primary		Secondary
· Shared files	Secondary	Primary		
Different-time / Different-place				
· Group writing	Secondary	Primary		
· Computer conferencing	Secondary	Primary		
· Conversational structuring	Secondary	Primary		
· Forms management	Secondary	Primary		
· Group voice mail	Secondary	Primary		

Table 17.2
Primary Groupware Users to Be Trained

Groupware	Team Members and Leaders	Professional Meeting Facilitator or Leader
Same time / Same place		
• Electronic copyboard		Primary
• PC projectors		Primary
• Group decision rooms		Primary
• Polling systems		Primary
Same time / Different place		
• Conference calls	Primary	
• Screen sharing	Primary	
• Video teleconferencing	Primary	
Different time / Same place		
• Team rooms		Primary
• Shared files	Primary	
Different time / Different place		
• Group writing	Primary	
• Computer conferencing	Primary	
• Conversational structuring	Primary	
• Forms management	Primary	
• Group voice mail	Primary	

sheets," or use of the technology itself to deliver training may be adequate.

Support people need even more substantive training than team leaders or members themselves. Through training, the end state is to institutionalize support—make it available where and when needed (see Table 17.2). Consequently, training on how to

Figure 17.1
4-Square Map of Groupware Options

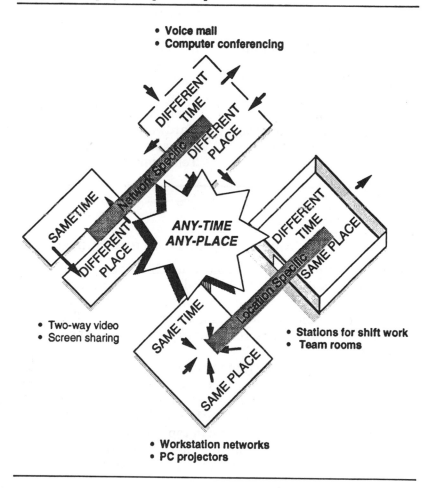

provide support may be needed for corporate and local information systems/telecommunications/facilities services. In some cases, even the local secretary who makes arrangements to hold a meeting in a particular room will need to be trained.

Initial and ongoing support runs the gamut from defining user needs, to servicing equipment, to providing telephone support (see "Groupware Training and Support Services").

Groupware Training and Support Services

Needs assessment
Functional specification
   development and solution
   selection
Pilot implementation and
   evaluation
Implementation planning
Site inspection and planning
Configuration (network,
   hardware, software)

System development/system
   integration
Management education on
   benefits and pitfalls
End user/team training
Documentation and media
   subscription services
Hardware maintenance
Software maintenance
Telephone support

Using the Technology to Train and Support

The beauty of groupware is that so much of the technology can be "bootstrapped"—actually be used to deliver training or support. The first time you use some form of groupware, you may need personal guidance in turning on or logging on. Thereafter, you can be trained by onscreen tutorials or intelligent computer-based training.

Examples of bootstrapping abound. Farallon Computer of Albany, California, runs its entire company supported by electronic mail. New employees learn company procedures through the mail system. With Farallon's screen-sharing product, Timbuktu, employees can tap experts anywhere in the company who can "lead a class" from their locations. Voice mail training at Aetna Life & Casualty comes from tutorials available at each step of operation. Sears orients users to video teleconferencing with a one-hour live conference in which an expert describes what video teleconferencing is, the benefits to business users, how to operate the technology, and the interpersonal skills best suited to it.

The best example of using the technology to provide support is augmentation (or even replacement) of telephone support with an AI-based expert support system. Such systems collect solutions to problems and make these available to users as answers to their questions. The process of collecting and

Figure 17.2
Problem-Solution Model (Source: LYSIS)

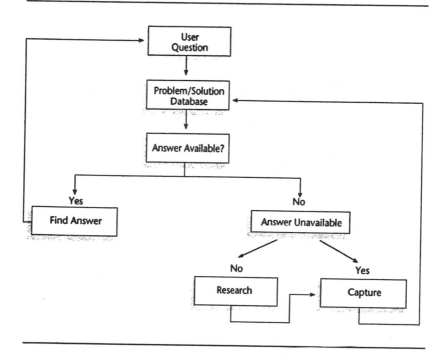

disseminating solutions to users typically follows the pattern depicted in Fig. 17.2.

Integrating Groupware Training and Support

A member of one of the teams we studied moaned, "Why does Information Systems treat me like a dummy when they're leading me off to the wilderness?" His lament is evidence that many information systems people introduce new technologies without helping the user understand how to apply the technology effectively. Office automation succeeded when the processes and work flows in offices were improved in preparation for the introduction of office technology. Similarly, gains in group performance will come from understanding group processes and improving them as groupware tools are deployed (see Fig 17.3).

Figure 17.3
Action Research Model

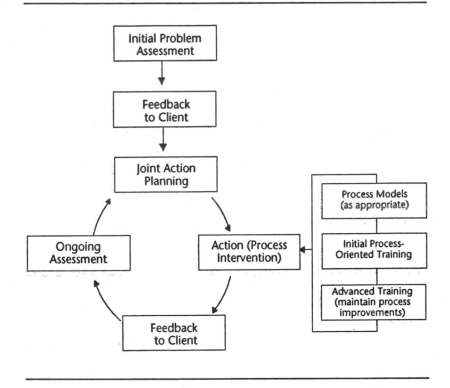

Thoughts on the Future of Training and Support

We believe that information systems and organization development (sometimes referred to as human resources, organization effectiveness, or industrial psychology) functions need to collaborate to provide the training and support organizationwide groupware requires. We'd like to see the creation of training and support teams with members from organization development, systems development, and end user computing groups. The teams' objectives would be to help workgroups and teams that show a genuine interest in moving to a connected workgroup environment, prepare a business case, and implement pilot projects. We'd like to see users have a single point of contact for electronic and nonelectronic groupware support. We are beginning to hear of companies with information systems organizations who have organization development or organization effectiveness experts or staff working alongside the technology experts. With a single point of contact, the business team can get whatever training and support is needed—be it technology or process-oriented support.

References

1. W. Bowen. "The puny payoff from office computers." *Fortune* (May 26, 1986): 20–24.

18

Of Pilots, Power Plants, and Pinstripes

*Groupware Lessons from
High-Performance Teams*

Some teams that work under the greatest pressure are not general business teams at all but teams working in specialized, critical areas. Air traffic controllers, military command and control officers, airplane pilots and navigators, medical operating room teams, electrical power plant and power dispatch center personnel—all are involved in mission-critical operations that depend on very effective team work.

These specialized teams have a strong sense of mission—they keep power flowing, planes flying, and people alive. Their objectives are very clear: success with no surprises. The performance of these teams is quite measurable, and their failures—plane crashes, failed surgeries, and blackouts—are very visible. Because the teams function in more closed environments, many of them follow a set of formal procedures. The functions of these teams are so critical that organizations are willing to invest heavily in training, support, and equipment for them.

Despite the constant pressure and higher stakes, there are many similarities between these teams and others. Each of these teams must

- communicate information within and outside the team,
- be clear about roles and goals,
- make decisions and allocate resources,
- face the same interpersonal conflicts as other teams,

- deal with losing old members and bringing in new members, and
- fight boredom and burnout.

These specialized teams provide meaningful lessons for many types of teams. Below are a few lessons particularly relevant to business teams.

Groupware Systems Must Provide Accurate Information

Teams require accurate information about the world around them. Power plant operators are trained to believe the gauges around them, but malfunctioning instruments deceived operators of the Three Mile Island power plant before its notorious accident. It was only when the operators checked on the actual equipment that they realized the magnitude of the problem and took corrective action. Groupware systems must not only give team members accurate information but also should provide a means of verifying its accuracy.

Handoffs Are Critical

The largest potential for breakdown occurs when responsibility for an item passes from one part of a team to another. At this point, the item can fall through the cracks or its status can be miscommunicated. The handoff may occur when a task is finished, with a change in status—such as a shift change—or when an airplane passes from one air space to another. Specialized teams spend a lot of resources on managing handoffs.

Hardware and Software Integration Are Important

As a team becomes responsible for more functions, it is tempting to add hardware and software tools to automate those functions. Some specialized teams find that the number of tools increases beyond a reasonable number. In one power plant control room, for example, operators must consult four separate workstations—one each to monitor fuel temperature, one to monitor steam temperature, another to assess plant performance, and a fourth to analyze combustion products. Additional workstations are planned to monitor recirculating water temperatures and to represent alarms. Business teams face a similar phenomenon of overload as new computer tools become available. The solution is costly and difficult—integration of tools into systems as they are built.

Breakdowns Occur in Complex Situations

Members of a team must maintain what industrial psychologists call situational awareness—they must see the big picture first, then understand the details. Situational awareness is most likely to break down under complex and changing conditions. AWACS (advance warning and control system) controllers are trained to give pilots successively less detailed information and orders as their own situations become overloaded. Under confusing and anomalous conditions, some controllers have lost control and had very strong emotional responses. Business situations are less dramatic, but they are substantially more complex than those of most specialized teams. Groupware tools should help reinforce the big picture and give levels of detail as they are needed.

Training, Training, Training

Specialized teams undergo extensive training on using the technologies that support them. Many have continuing training and certification to keep skills honed. Some businesses view training as a costly nuisance. For high-performance business teams, it may be a key to their success.[1]

References

1. See Chapter 17, "Sustainable Benefits Come from Training and Support."

19

How to Tell When a Team's in Trouble

Danger Signals to Watch For

As team leader, you're in charge. Others may help plan or implement, but you're the one accountable for the results of the team. When you don't get results—or even when you do but think the team could perform better—how do you identify the team's problems? In this article, we discuss some indications of team trouble. If you're thinking of implementing groupware, you had best address the following problems first.

Organizational Difficulties

Teams exist within organizations, and organizations exist within a business and cultural environment. External environmental

shifts, such as a change in the economy, regulations, or competition, can put your team in hot water. You could lose management support, as your "team champion" turns his or her interest to counteracting these environmental changes. Or these perturbations may cause a dramatic change in your team makeup or charter. The result could be that the resources to get the team's tasks done dwindle away.

> *Example:* A cross-division team responsible for developing an organizationwide strategy lost its authority to make decisions when its market dramatically declined—only corporate management would define strategy in this situation. The company reorganized into fewer divisions, and this team lost two managers as their products were moved to another division. All momentum toward defining a corporate strategy was lost.

Leadership Problems

 You could be the cause of your team's troubles! Periodically you may need to reflect on your leadership style. Is it appropriate for the nature of the work to be done or for the maturity of your team members? Are you out of synch with the needs of the others on your team? Are you too task-oriented, not paying enough attention to interpersonal behavior? Are you so focused on the content of your team's work that you don't pay attention to the process for developing and delivering content?

> *Example:* The team leader, an ex-school teacher, was used to giving orders, expecting everyone to accomplish their tasks his way. Yet the team members were all experienced managers with creative ideas of their own. Members constantly rebelled against his directive style, causing him to

become even more heavy-handed. We expected to see him pull out a hickory stick and whack heads!

Interpersonal Conflicts

As Red Barber says, "If you've got two sports fans, you've got at least three opinions." With two or more people in a group, you've got differences of opinions, styles, speeds of working, levels of education and experience, and ways of learning—all of which can result in interpersonal conflicts. Power plays can erupt or a team can mutiny, which is frequently the case when a leader prefers one method of performing and everyone else can't use that method or doesn't want to. Eventually the members lose faith in the leader and start working their own way. Whatever the cause, interpersonal conflicts lead to a loss of productivity.

> *Example:* Two project leaders manage a large team with the charter of developing new management training. One leader thinks she could have managed the project; she is jealous of the other. She gets her work done on time; the other doesn't. She blows up, and the entire team suffers. She watches every move of the other project leader, and if he makes the slightest wrong decision in her perception, she's immediately on the phone to her boss. Tension mounts and the team's work is disrupted.

Group Interactions

The ways all members interact with each other and with the leader are ripe with potential rottenness. As a group, everyone may focus on the tasks at hand and ignore group processes such as building trust, goal clarification, and decision-making, essential to high performance. On the other hand, they may focus on their group process to the detriment of actually doing the work, which is the reason for their existence.

Group members can engage in "invalid orneriness" or "bad fights." A good fight surfaces constructive conflict, which results in a solution; a bad fight is an argument not related to the purpose of the team.

> *Example:* In meetings, group members practice "in and out" behavior. At no time is the entire team in a meeting;

rather, individuals run out to make telephone calls, get forgotten material, talk to others, or go to the bathroom—anything to keep them from focusing on what the team needs to accomplish in a meeting or from being present when commitments must be made.

Or they practice "avoidance behavior" or "volunteer behavior." Avoidance behavior is evidenced by everyone averting their eyes when the leader makes a request. Volunteer behavior is when everyone volunteers for more and more tasks. The first results in the tasks not getting done; the second does too, as people become overcommitted and unable to meet deadlines.

Finally, the group can engage in "groupthink." People say what they think the leader and others want to hear—within the group. Unfortunately, outside the team, they may express their true feelings and beliefs and counteract the work of the team.

> *Example:* Members of a small start-up publishing company amazed themselves when they released their first magazine within budget and ahead of schedule. The second issue sweetened the taste of success with praise from local critics. By the third issue, everyone saw signs of trouble brewing, but no one talked about them. Within a year, short tempers and high stress were more characteristic of this team than a quality arts and entertainment magazine. Everyone wondered what had happened, but still no one talked about it.

Individual Behavior

Individuals' behavioral idiosyncrasies also can derail a team. One member may be completely silent in a meeting but criticize outside. Some members are never prepared for meetings, or consistently miss deadlines. Each may have a personal agenda that overrides his or her effectiveness as a team member. One person may just not understand what needs to be done; he or she can't follow procedures.

> *Example:* In a cross-product line marketing team, each member found it difficult, if not impossible, to set aside his or her product line concerns to participate effectively in

"It's a distress signal. She's trying to tell us her work station has shut down."

the umbrella group. In another group, one male member was constantly harassing the women, trying to get a date. The women were furious—but unwilling to confront his inappropriate behavior.

Equipment Difficulties

The best indicator that a team's use of groupware is in trouble is if the equipment is consistently broken. Short of that, there are lots of other indications of trouble. On the one hand, groupware use can drop off after an initial period of enthusiastic use. On the other hand, team members can become so enamored of the tool that they don't accomplish their team's objectives. Or one member may not use a groupware tool, causing difficulties for everyone else.

> *Example:* One member of a team using electronic mail refused to read his mail every day, forcing an exception to the agreed upon way of communicating. In another team supported by electronic mail, the distribution list did not reflect the full membership of the team, making electronic

mail an exclusive tool, rather than using it to achieve free information flow among team members.

If you see evidence of team trouble along a number of different lines, we offer just one prescription: See your doctor! Get help from an internal or external expert—a process consultant, a meeting facilitator, an organizational development consultant or, in the case of trouble with groupware, from an expert groupware implementer.

The Danger Signals of Team Trouble

Team produces no results or wrong results
Team members mutiny
Excessive miscommunications/misunderstandings
One individual consistently disrupts the team
Coalitions within the group consistently disrupt the team
Deadlines are consistently missed
Members are bored or burned out
Equipment is consistently broken

20

Hoshin

Thinking Further, Japanese Style

Hoshin is a term derived from Japanese Total Quality practices, itself inspired in part by American gurus such as W. Edwards Deming, Phillip Crosby, Joseph Juran, and others[1] (see Chapter 9,"TQ Groupware"). Literally translated as "to advance," hoshin refers to the concept of "policy deployment" or (more expressively) "pointing direction for management." A hoshin is a very long-term goal that is shared across an entire organization.

Hoshin typically emerge from "bottom-up" da__ llection from all employees that identifies options and deve' __ consensus. Top management must participate in this proc__ in such a

way that their involvement supports but does not dominate the overall process. And top management must buy into the results.

Over 20 years ago, Honda established a hoshin of becoming number one in customer satisfaction in the U.S. automobile market, and it developed specific methods for measuring and evaluating how it would go about it. Another example is Florida Power and Light, one of the American success stories in the use of quality techniques. FPL stated its hoshin thus: "to reduce the frequency and duration of electric outages to Western Division customers."

After the hoshin are set, "presidential audits" (sometimes called "management audits" or "quality visits") are used to sustain the hoshin process over a period of time. During these visits, senior executives go around and ask, "How can I help you achieve these hoshin?" It is important to realize that, in Japan, such visits are an audit of the executive who is visiting—not an evaluation of the employees being visited.

In our experience, the term hoshin is used in many different ways by U.S. companies. Most American hoshin we have seen tend to be quite short term in orientation (certainly not 20 years) and almost indistinguishable from a management-by-objectives approach. We suspect that the idea of a 20-year goal that is single-mindedly pursued by the entire company is simply too difficult for most American companies to swallow and—even if swallowed—to digest.

References

1. W.E. Deming. *Out of the Crisis.* Cambridge, Mass.: Massachusetts Institute of Technology, Center for Advanced Engineering Study, 1988; P.B. Crosby. *Quality Is Free: The Art of Making Quality Certain.* New York: Mentor Books, 1979; J.M. Juran (ed.) *Quality Control Handbook.* New York: McGraw-Hill, 1974; See also, for example, J. Cullen and J. Hollingum. *Implementing Total Quality.* Bedford, UK: IFS Publications, Ltd., 1987; and L.S. Richman. "Software catches the team spirit." *Fortune* (June 8, 1987): 125–133.

21

Seeding Serendipitous Groups

Serendipity—An Aptitude for Making Fortunate Discoveries Accidentally

 A key trait for many high-per-formance teams is how they seem to come together almost by accident. Often the groups themselves view their position within their companies as a "skunkworks"—an organi-zation working on the fringe of any official charter and without support of traditional infrastructures. More often than not, the success of these groups results as much from serendipitous coincidences as it does from a top-down management plan: Two would-be team members happen to meet, or the team chances across another piece of the puzzle elsewhere in the company. When a group is really operating in sync, valuable things just seem to fall into their laps.

No matter how good a group is, serendipitous good fortune seems essential to its eventual success. One cannot plan seren-dipitous encounters, but judicious use of groupware technologies can make it more likely that they will occur. One way of thinking about this challenge is to break the range of possible approaches into passive and active serendipitous schemes.

E-mail is a key serendipitous technology that can be either passive or active. The presence of an E-mail system encourages spontaneous communications across organizations and organi-zational lines. A simple electronic-mail system is passive in that it is a simple conduit for communications. Add a conferencing capability and set up conferences around topic areas in which the company is seeking innovation, and it becomes more active.

An example of E-mail in its most active configuration is Bellcore's advisor program, which actively matches potential advisors with those who need their expertise. A similar approach could be used to provide external support for teams at critical stages, or even to encourage teams to form by linking like-minded entrepreneurs.

A key challenge for E-mail is teaching managers to accept "waste"—seemingly irrelevant communications—as the cost of uncovering relevant and important nuggets that bring groups together. E-mail–based conferencing, in particular, can cultivate serendipitous connections, both at the formation stage and later, when groups are seeking outside connections.

Another challenge stems from the fact that the happenstance nature of many teams means they do not typically have access to extensive groupware resources. More often than not, such groups learn to make do with whatever is already available in their organizations. Companies can do much to cultivate serendipity by simply ensuring that basic groupware structures such as E-mail, voice mail, or conference room technologies are available within the company.

Ultimately, though, the key to cultivating serendipity is not the technology per se, but the approach to using the technology. Accepting "failures" and some waste is essential to the process. Finding ways for new groups to use technology in idiosyncratic ways is an important strategy. For example, a company could keep a small number of group support technologies (copyboards, laptop computers, etc.) available in a central pool to be checked out by participants. Simply keeping a record of which groups check out the resources could provide important information on overall corporate innovation health.

22

Team Mania Hits Corporate Executives

Mania: (1) excitement manifested by mental and physical hyperactivity, disorganization of behavior, and elevation of mood; (2) excessive or unreasonable enthusiasm.

The concept of "teams" has cannonballed into the lexicon of senior executive buzzwords. Such rapidly increasing popularity is not surprising: These small, cross-organizational, time-driven, task-focused workgroups provide a practical form of bureaucratic bypass. Successful business teams can put numbers up on the board quickly.

Teams have received the Peter Drucker seal of approval, as administered in a *Harvard Business Review* article[1] that set a reprint record for the magazine and later became a chapter in the book *The New Realities.*[2] The team wave is swelling with the appearance of popular business features such as the *Business Week* cover story called "Go Team!"[3] and the special issue of the Conference Board's *Across the Board* called "Catch the Team Spirit."[4] Teams, it appears, are on everyone's mind as they dream about (or dread) the organization of the future.

Japan is a major source of credibility for business team proponents. Business teams are legendary in Japan. They are historically linked to overarching concepts like Total Quality (à la W. Edwards Deming, Joseph Juran, et al.)[5] and long-term perspectives like the notion of hoshin (see Chapter 20, "Hoshin"). Business teams work in Japan because they have become an integral part of the larger business and cultural worldview of that country, and an effective means for implementing its long-term goals.

In the United States, however, interest in business teams seems to be fueled more by the need for a quick fix than by the quest for long-term solutions. In this era of mergers and acquisitions, deregulation, stock market turmoil, and intense international competition, short-term financials are on everyone's mind—whether explicitly or implicitly. Business teams are fast on their feet, so they play well in short-term financial games. But will the diverse actions of many different teams, each pursuing its own short-term goals, be orchestrated for the long-term corporate good?

Our fear is that a team mania is in the offing for many American companies, and it is quite possible that individual business teams will achieve their own goals but fail to work together to reach enterprisewide goals. The result could be an organizational explosion sparked by hundreds of well intentioned—and even high performing—business teams.

What is needed is macro-level glue to hold together the micro-level energies of business teams. A coordination theory (now being pursued by researchers in Tom Malone's new center at MIT,[6] as well as at a few other universities) could provide a conceptual foundation for such action. Beyond theory, specific management approaches must be developed to exploit the creativity and speed of action inherent in business teams, while channeling this energy into enterprisewide and long-term goals. Groupware tools can help make such management approaches possible and practical.

Business teams now have passed the public relations threshold of senior management in the United States. But it is critical to create American business teams that capture both short-term and long-term benefits. Team mania is avoidable, but only if we act quickly to realize the promises of business teams and avoid their pitfalls.

References

1. P.F. Drucker. "The coming of the new organization." *Harvard Business Review* (January–February 1988):45–53.

2. P.F. Drucker. *The New Realities*. New York: Harper and Row, 1989.

3. J. Hoerr. "The payoff from teamwork." *Business Week* (July 10, 1989):56

4. "Catch the team spirit: The great experiment in team management." *Across the Board* 26(May 1989):5.

5. W.E. Deming. *Out of the Crisis*. Cambridge, Mass.: Massachusetts Institute of Technology, Center for Advanced Engineering Study, 1988. J.M. Juran (ed.). *Quality Control Handbook*. New York: McGraw-Hill, 1974. P.B. Crosby. *Quality Is Free: The Art of Making Quality Certain*. New York: Mentor Books, 1979. See also J. Cullen and J. Hollingum. *Implementing Total Quality*. Bedford, U.K.: IFS Publications, Ltd., 1987; and J. R. Hauser and D. Clausing. "The house of quality." *Harvard Business Review* (May–June 1988):63–73.

6. T.W. Malone. *What Is Coordination Theory?* Cambridge, Mass.: Massachusetts Institute of Technology. Paper presented at the National Science Foundation Coordination Theory Workshop, February 19, 1988. See also T.W. Malone, et al. "Intelligent information-sharing systems." *Communications of the ACM* 30(1987)5:390–402; and T.W. Malone, et al. "Semistructured messages are surprisingly useful for computer-supported coordination." *ACM Transactions on Office Information Systems* 5(1987)2:115–131.

Part IV
Groupware in Practice

23

Magnus Corporation

A Composite Case Study

During the Groupware Users' Project, a series of pilot tests were conducted with teams in diverse industry sectors. This composite case study was assembled from those tests. We worked closely with the teams represented in this case study in two ways.

- First, we were consultants on group process, recommending and advising on both electronic groupware tools and process methodologies.

"When they asked if I wanted to participate in a same-time/same-place groupware project, this isn't what I had in mind."

- Second, we tracked the teams' experiences as they tested out various forms of groupware. We interviewed with team members at various points during the trial and used the Team Performance Inventory to provide valid data on a team's strengths and weaknesses.

This case study provides a mirror for seeing early challenges in groupware use in the real world. The company specifics have been disguised and are drawn from several different pilots, but the experiences are real. In order to generalize in a systematic way, we are using the Team Performance Model as a framework for summarizing this case study (see Chapter 2, "Mapping the Groupware Territory").

Linking Goals and Information

Origins of the Project

In December of 1987, Magnus Corporation, a large manufacturing and service company, initiated a Technology Planning Process (TPP) aimed at linking business goals and uses of information systems. The vision for this process was that it would be enterprisewide, crossing the many divisions of this diversified company, and that it would serve as a force varied to integrate efforts and establish competitive advantages in the many markets where Magnus Corporation is active.

The Technology Planning Process (TPP) began formally when Kevin Franklin, a senior manager within Magnus Corporation, asked Jack White, a well known "intrapreneur" with a remarkable track record for introducing new ideas and new technology, to take on a new project. At the time of his assignment, Jack was given a very broad (and very vague) mandate—to do something about technology planning and implementation, so that projects didn't self-cancel and systems work could integrate with the larger company strategies. He had no team assigned to work with him. He had access to resources, but primarily through informal channels—which he was very used to playing from previous assignments. Jack was an aggressive leader who knew how to get things done. He commented, "I use the hallways a lot," and he meant both the hallways of the corporate buildings and the electronic hallways available via LINK, the company's large electronic messaging system.

Firming up the Mandate

Jack surveyed many people and wrote several proposals that outlined a sweeping project to align the TPP with company strategies enterprisewide. He found a champion in one of the top systems managers and began shopping around for outside approaches—management decided early on not to invent it all in-house. Technology planning was inserted on the agenda of a special offsite meeting of top technology managers. Jack found that everyone inside and outside was talking about the same problems: the need for a systematic way of evaluating and implementing new technology, as well as for achieving system integration.

Jack recruited 40 to 50 planners from the at-large organization to help implement the project. A core group screened proposals from outside vendors, clarified goals, and selected IBIS, a comprehensive technology-planning methodology that was strategically oriented. The firm that had developed IBIS was invited to give a presentation to senior management. The presentation, however, raised more questions among senior managers than answers. Thus, just as Jack headed into his first "turn" in the team performance cycle (Commitment: Stage 4), top management had second thoughts. A series of memo loops in April resulted in a vastly downsized project for Jack. Meeting after meeting was held with the planners to renegotiate their involvement. Finally, in early May a letter of agreement with the IBIS developers was signed and the formal project, in its pared-down form, began.

Jack was disappointed but not daunted. The new mandate marked out a technology transfer objective: to test the IBIS approach with two parallel teams, one working within the corporate systems group, and one working with the functional entities on the business side of the company. Core teams of planners were recruited to this mandate in early June. Figure 23.1 shows, in general, the work undertaken. Since the two teams themselves followed the Team Performance Model, the model is used to summarize the learnings about groupware which we gleaned as the Technology Planning Project progressed.

Magnus Corporation
Technology Planning Process (TPP)

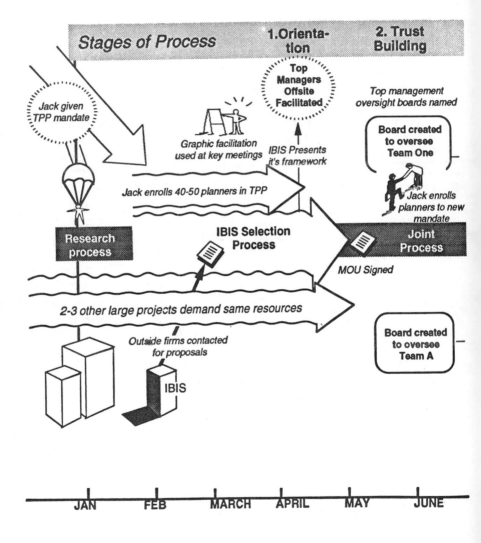

Magnus Corporation's Technology Planning Process (TPP)

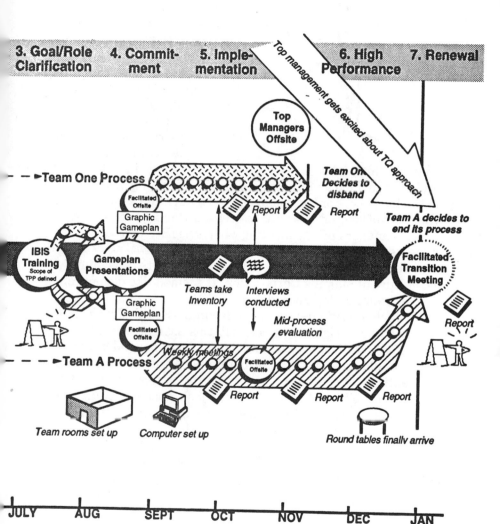

Stage 1: Orientation

Orienting this team was no easy matter, because the vision of integrating technology planning with company strategy was specified only in approximate terms, and was greatly reduced in scope from the original concept, due to senior management concerns.

The decision to go with the IBIS methodology supported the team's orientation, since the methodology—packaged very visibly in a large ring binder—provided an important sense of grounding. However, the methodology was only a cookbook; the team still needed to decide what sort of "menu" it would be creating during the pilot. At the senior managers' offsite meeting where the IBIS method was first presented, the heavily analytical nature of the IBIS process made clear that it would have to be adapted to be more consistent with the culture of Magnus Corporation. It seemed like a comprehensive, but adaptable, methodology.

Jack recruited two team leaders—Kevin Franklin (his boss, who had originally given him this assignment) and Jerry Largo, both well connected managers. Jerry headed Team One, which would look at the information needs of the various business entities of the company outside the systems group. Kevin would head Team A, which would look specifically at needs within the information systems group, the host for the project. The many negotiations Jack had with the technology planners, or "planners" as they came to be called, had helped orient them to the need for the project. But questions about scope were not clear. Many on Team One were asking the Stage 1/Orientation question "Why am I here?" and not getting a good answer. Some had been directed to join.

Most members of Team A, on the other hand, saw obvious benefits in learning about the IBIS methodology, even if the project didn't succeed as planned. Everyone seemed willing to be there, although only half actually volunteered. Only a few were clearly uncomfortable with being involved in the effort.

Both Jack and Kevin hoped the project would have a direct impact on the business at large and that it would help build bridges to the business entities (within the company) for the systems people.

Even before specific team members were completely assigned, a four-day training session in the IBIS methodology was initiated. Thus, just as people were asking "Why am I here?" the conscious focus of the group (still not a team, but the group from which team members were selected) was on the new methodology the teams would be using. These people were being trained, in quite a rigid fashion, as "planners"; they were trying out a new set of skills and—to some extent—a new identity as a planner.

In retrospect, this instant immersion in content was probably not a good idea. The classic Stage 1/Orientation concerns about overall purpose were postponed without comment in order to pursue the details (and there were many details) of the new methodology. Jack's low-key charisma kept everyone pretty quiet but not very confident.

Shortly thereafter, as the teams were meeting on their own following the initial training offsite, the "Why am I here?" questions surfaced with great vigor and some hostility. The IBIS methodology and its pervasive structures drew most of the attention in the early stages, leaving many orientation issues unresolved. This lack of resolution had come back to haunt the team leaders.

Lessons Learned Regarding Orientation

1. Team leadership style is a critical element in orientation, as the style of this team leader revealed.

2. Changes of scope and uncertainty in mandates from the larger organization are fundamentally destabilizing. Team A, working within the systems areas, trusted its mandate from Jack. Team One, with its assignment to work with the business areas, got a mixed message when the scope changed. When people can't adequately answer purpose questions, they tend to withdraw from the team development process.

3. Introducing a preset methodology for use by a team has real trade-offs. Anchors are useful, but not if they hold you back when you're ready to move.

4. Simple graphic templates (that can be created and used by nonartists) can have surprisingly high value as orienting aids. Simple graphics seem to be an important orientation aid that people respond to quickly.

5. "Big picture" graphic techniques (to remind team members about overall directions and issues) are important to keep a group oriented while in the midst of complex data-gathering and analysis activities.

6. The mechanics and logistics of setting up a team room for high performance take much longer than expected.

7. The "clubhouse effect" may be the most important value of having a team room, even though specific components also add great value.

8. It is important for a team to have slogans at the "bumper sticker" level to remind themselves and others about their central mandate.

Groupware Used for Stage 1: Orientation

Team Meetings

Face-to-face meeting was the fundamental groupware tool used throughout the Technology Planning Process, especially at the beginning. Both teams met weekly to review progress.

The IBIS Technology Planning Methodology

This became the structure through which the teams were working during the pilot. It was, in effect, a form of groupware—because each team worked through it. Although the methodology was revised as they went, its essential structure held and shaped the teams in profound ways.

A Team Room

Each team was assigned a room that would be its own for the life of the pilot. The room played an important orientation function within the process of meetings. It reminded team members, during their weekly team meetings and ad hoc meetings, of their overall effort as a team. "We could pick up where we left off at the last meeting, instantly." The team room also gave a sense of the importance to what the team was doing. It was viewed as evidence of "implied acceptance" by management of their work. From the start, these teams felt that they had the power to get things done, and the assignment of the team room was one expression of this power.

LINK Electronic Messaging

Team members were signed onto the electronic network and a special conference was created for the project. In the beginning, Jack used this adeptly to get people focused on the reasons for the work and its importance to Magnus Corporation.

Graphic Displays

At the orientation off site, Jack made a presentation to all the top managers about the project with the assistance of a graphic facilitator who created a large concept drawing of the overall Technology Planning Process. This orienting imagery helped people understand the project initially, and it became a critical groupware tool during the Team A process. IBIS also used graphic displays integrally with its methodology.

Off-site Meetings

The initial methodology training session was conducted as an off-site meeting; there were also several others during the pilot period. The team members commented that the off-site meetings were important to "re-energize," "refocus," and "humanize" the team process. The off-site meetings provided an important forum for orientation, trust-building, goal clarification, and commitment issues.

Facilitators

During the pilot, outside facilitators were used for most of the off-site meetings. In addition, a team member was assigned to play this role during regular meetings. The designated facilitator had the effect of reminding people of the overall direction of the team and could orient or reorient as appropriate. Applying facilitation resources to the project also underlined its importance.

Stage 2: Trust Building

For both teams, trust building happened primarily during the personal enrollment process that Jack conducted, and during the initial "shape-up" meetings of the teams. Some members were not sure what motivations might be driving Kevin and Jack (who both attended Team A's meetings) to become involved in the TPP. Kevin and Jack themselves were nervous after the shift in scope. Would the business side support the process they were introducing? Aligning technology-planning efforts in the various parts of the company would require major cooperation.

For those team members who knew Jack's work and were excited about having the chance to work with him, trust was immediate—and energizing. For those who had not known him previously, there were uncertainties about his entrepreneurial style. On Team One, which had more members who were sent to the project, Jerry Largo was not immediately perceived to be an instant success as a leader. He was very knowledgeable, but not good at keeping focus. In fact, he was not anxious to assume leadership of the team. Given some of the start-up confusion on scope, and his not being a direct part of the TPP process initially, he was not in a good position to develop or keep control.

Appointment of two oversight boards led to some trust that the process would be taken seriously, but this appointment also could have been taken the other way. The external trust issue ultimately proved to be the most critical and difficult to manage. (We suspect that wrestling with such external factors will become increasingly common for teams in large, diverse corporations.)

The cross-organizational responsibilities of the team members were the major source of trust problems. As mentioned earlier, most of the members of both TPP teams had other responsibilities and "another boss" to worry about. In some cases, the mandate from that other boss (often perceived as the real boss) was not supportive or at least not clear regarding the mandate of the TPP. Such a situation raised trust issues indirectly, but they had to be resolved within the team, which was often difficult to do.

During the later Goal/Role Clarification stage, when each group was creating game plans for their work, Team A returned to the trust issue and discussed at some length what the personal agendas were for each member of the team. This was actually recorded on a Game Plan Chart, which will be described later, and led to a high level of interpersonal bonding on the team. Some members of Team A also knew each other well from prior work. They reported a high sense of trust within the team during later evaluations. They felt they could speak their minds and felt that team members were being candid with each other. There was a high degree of give and take among the team members.

Even though all of the team members on both teams were long-term employees of Magnus Corporation, they did not have experience with all the varied parts of the corporation. Consequently, substantial differences in terminology and perspectives had to be worked through. Many apparently personal differences in the early phases of the teams were actually traceable to differences in language. For example, the word "sell" was positive to some members but negative to others. In order to avoid time-consuming "bad fights" (when team members fight about something with regard to which there is really more commonality than division), the facilitators kept reminding the team about clarification of terminology. This problem would have been even more intense if the team members came from more diverse backgrounds. In fact, these team members were quite similar in many ways, yet the language differences were significant and often slowed the team's work.

The involvement of the outside methodology and consultants had a mixed impact regarding trust. On the one hand, there was a tendency to trust the methodology, since it had been selected through a competitive process and was endorsed by the team leader—who had led the competitive review of methodologies. On the other hand, the complexity of the methodology, combined with the fact that everyone tended to know at least something about strategic technology planning (and some areas of the corporation already had their own methods), led team members to be somewhat distrustful of the overall process—and thus of the team. This type of indirectly inspired mistrust was tricky to deal with, although it was not very intense and thus did not create great problems.

Lessons Learned Regarding Trust Building

1. Trust within the team is often influenced by factors that are outside the scope or control of the team, particularly within corporations that have matrix structures or other forms of cross-organizational responsibilities.

2. Packaged methodologies can relieve some trust issues, but they can also raise or paper over other ones.

3. Trust in a leader can sometimes supersede mistrust of other team members. It can also work in reverse.

4. It is very difficult for any groupware tools to handle trust issues directly. This is an issue involving feelings, motivations, and a sense of whether or not the overall progress is productive. Tools that provide encouraging feedback can build trust.

Groupware Used for Stage 2: Trust Building

Team Meetings

Weekly team meetings were the forums within which most of the trust building occurred. The facilitator on the team consciously helped this process along. On Team One the trust issues focused on Largo, as resistant team members increasingly questioned the value of trying to get business entities to cooperate. On Team A, the trust built strongly with the repeated meetings.

Off-site Meetings

The periodic off-site meetings also played a role here, as did person-to-person work between meetings. Both the facilitator and the team leader played important roles.

Valid Data on Group Process

The graphic facilitation techniques of the external consultants increased trust that everyone was being heard. Mid-process administration of the Drexler/Sibbet/Forrester Team Performance Inventory also indicated the team members' trust of each other. These results were then fed back to team members and discussed.

Stage 3: Goal/Role Clarification

Two IBIS training off-site meetings were the key settings for Goal and Role Clarification during the project. The first off-site meeting was totally devoted to the IBIS method. The second involved each team meeting alone and then presenting a game plan for its implementation stages to the combined groups. Although this second meeting took both groups right into commitment concerns, the goal and role clarification process was still continuing.

New groupware possibilities were introduced at this stage. The IBIS methodology itself called for computer support for the organizational analyses that were being undertaken by the teams. The teams also had a green light to occupy two small conference rooms in corporate headquarters. Discussions about how to equip the rooms focused talk about goals. Team A concluded it needed a copyboard to reproduce wall graphics easily. The LINK conferences also were organized.

All of this discussion was compressed into one meeting held in preparation for the second IBIS training. The idea of using the Team Performance Model as a framework for talking about team processes was introduced. The facilitators suggested

Figure 23.2
Game Plan

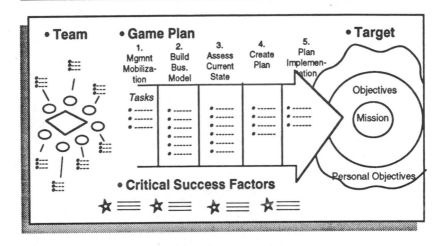

creating graphic game plans articulating the mission and goals of the team, its major stages and tasks, and its own critical success factors (see Fig. 23.2). The chart was used to report to the combined group the following day. In one activity, the team reviewed Orientation, Trust Building, Goal/Role Clarification and Commitment issues that they were encountering.

Team A (whose meetings Kevin Franklin and Jack White both attended) was able to clarify and commit to a mission and objectives fairly easily, although considerable discussion occurred about how the specific scope related to ways of outlining the area they would plan for. Team A also found that creating a team profile was exciting, because the team involved key players within the systems group at corporate. Spelling out the major phases and tasks gave people a clear sense of the work they were doing, and the discussion of critical success factors began preparing them for implementation and high performance.

Team One had a tougher time. They did not get beyond discussions of the mission and objectives in their first meeting—which lasted for several painful hours. Many members were skeptical about the value of the whole effort. They weren't getting the support they needed from their bosses and suspected that the work could come to a dead end. They trusted each other as individuals well enough, but they didn't trust the process. They were less familiar with Jack, who ended up attending most of their meetings and tried desperately to patch the team together. The initial problems with orientation and trust were never solved for Team One, and midway through the pilot the team felt it had accomplished what the pilot had set out to do—which was to test the IBIS methodology on the business side—and it disbanded. In a sense, they declared a victory in a war they had decided they could not win.

Within both teams, goal clarification at a more specific level was typically done during the weekly team meetings. Written goals were done on flip charts or newsprint (sometimes a copyboard was used for this purpose). Copies of agreed-upon goals were made and distributed. These sessions were very spirited exchanges, with highly interactive discussions to clarify and refine goals as well as to sow the seeds of commitment within the team.

The leaders also used the LINK computer messaging system within the company to summarize what had been agreed upon at each team meeting. This medium was thus a form of commitment management, where agreements were published in electronic form for all the team members to see.

In spite of the rather changeable nature of the goals being pursued by the Technology Planning Project, there was relatively little confusion or misunderstanding regarding goals. The team members all reported a high degree of clarity, at least from the mid-point of the pilot on. Jack emphasized specificity in goals, and the various groupware tools that he used worked quite well to enforce this clarity.

Lessons Learned Regarding Goal Clarification

1. Goal clarification is an ongoing process; you cannot just do it and forget it.
2. The key groupware functionality for goal clarification is the ability to take a hard-copy record of what was agreed upon away from a meeting. Follow-up via electronic messaging can seal such agreements.
3. The specifics of goal clarification must be wrestled through during highly interactive meetings. Face to

face is probably best for such sessions but not essential if a team is well oriented and has high trust levels.

4. Conventional nonelectronic tools (for example, scissors and tape) are often most effective when the organizing pattern is not yet known, especially when combined with the intuition of skilled humans.

5. Immediate feedback (that is, *same time*) seems important at the goal and role clarification stage, to be sure one is being heard and to confirm what is going to happen.

Groupware Used for Stage 3: Goal Clarification

Flip Charts/Newsprint

The team room was lined with hanging flip charts and had room to roll out newsprint for recording as needed. These were used frequently to record goals and other plans. All the team members got involved in this process, although the facilitator did more of it that the other team members.

"Elevator Speeches"

During the first team meeting, the facilitators asked team members to share "elevator speeches" that they would use to describe what they were embarking on with the new team. The idea here is to assume that you had a brief elevator ride with a senior executive. How would you summarize, in a very few words, the important aspects of what your team is doing? This simple technique proved very effective in getting team members clear about the mission and objectives. It was also used during off-site meetings later in the pilot. Forcing people to summarize what they are doing is a surprisingly powerful group aid at the early stages in the life of a new team.

Copyboard

A copyboard was sometimes used for recording key agreements. It had the capability of copying flip charts and newsprint with a scanner bar, so team members could leave the team meeting with a hard-copy record of what had been agreed to. The team members were creative in making this medium work for them. They cut large rolls of newsprint from their standard size (using a giant bandsaw) to fit the copyboard so that large displays could be copied easily. The copyboard was used frequently for draft/ erase/redraft/erase/etc. exchanges, with a shared hard copy at the end of the session.

Computer Messaging

After team meetings, the team leader would circulate text summaries of new goals and what had been agreed to. There was typically little discussion of these summaries, but they served to firm up new goals and encourage commitment. Seeing the goals stated in text, distributed via LINK, provided an important tone of realism. It was important that all of the team members personally accessed the electronic messaging system at least once a day, so this was an established work habit that this team could build upon.

Scissors and Tape

One of the early strategic planning activities was to gather business goals and critical success factors (things that must go right for the business to succeed). The team leader took a list of all of the resulting goals and cut them up with scissors to group and rearrange. He then taped them together and reviewed them with the rest of the team. Even though this team had access to sophisticated computerized techniques for such activities, they found traditional scissors and tape—combined with the team leader's skills in synthesizing ideas—to be most effective.

Stage 4: Commitment/ Decision Making

This stage most clearly revealed both the strengths and weaknesses of adopting a formal methodology like the IBIS system. Because Team A had a lot of trust in Jack and in each other and were clear on their goals and the benefits to the corporate systems group (whether or not it succeeded), they breezed through the creating stages of team development and committed quickly to implementing the IBIS process.

Team One struggled with several sessions but eventually committed to doing the minimal number of interviews and analysis required to meet the specifications of the IBIS methodology.

In both cases the roles and responsibilities of team members were clearly defined, agreed upon, and communicated. The team members reported that they felt they were getting what they needed from resources outside their team—even though many felt they were getting mixed signals, especially from their own management. Everyone on the team agreed that they had developed an overall strategy to guide their team decision making. They felt they knew how to make decisions, and they made them.

Linkage with the larger organization and its commitment to the process was the more significant challenge. Both teams knew that managing top management commitments would be a key to any downstream implementation of their work. The changeable nature of the overall mission was frustrating. They still wanted to take on the expanded charter as originally conceived. This led to some anxieties and frustrations among the team members.

For example, with regard to the Team Performance Inventory (administered about halfway through the pilot period), there was strong consensus about which question most accurately expressed what they felt was the critical area for improving team performance. The item they selected read as follows: "I wouldn't be surprised if what our group produces is never used." There was a fear that the team would get to the end of the pilot and find a brick wall—in spite of their success.

Thus the commitment within the team seemed much stronger than what the team members perceived was the commitment of their managers. Such a situation functioned as a braking factor for the team, but there was no question that they wanted to go ahead anyway. A representative quote from a team member during interviews at the halfway point in the pilot: "We have to go on! If we stopped now, there would be value to the people who participated, but the organization hasn't gotten any value yet. If we stopped now, nothing would happen." These are the words of team members who had become fully committed to their cause, in spite of the fact that they weren't at all sure that their cause could succeed.

Commitment became a minor issue in equipping the team rooms. For example, the logistics of hanging flip charts, setting up storage areas, and so on, had to be handled by team members. The buildings and services people were no help and were, in fact, a major block. The round table requested at the beginning of the pilot did not arrive until the pilot was almost over, six months later. In spite of these difficulties and delays, major benefits of the team room were realized by virtue of simply having a regular place to call their own. In the case of Team A, one team member was assigned the role of setting up and maintaining the team room and the various electronic and nonelectronic aids in it. This was very useful; but, in retrospect, this person needed to be much more aggressive in making things happen quickly.

Lessons Learned Regarding Commitment/ Decision Making

1. Personal commitment to a leader or other team members is often more important to team performance than formal commitment from senior management.

2. At the commitment stage, in-person commitments can be powerful, but electronic follow-up is useful to confirm and has the effect of sealing the commitment.

3. Commitment is not an inherently difficult stage, if the early stages in the team performance cycle have gone well.

4. In spite of good team spirit and commitment, lack of organizational commitment outside the team can undermine performance in the end.

5. Immediate feedback (that is, *same time*) seems important at the commitment stage, in order to ensure that each team member understands what he or she is committing to do.

6. Buildings and services organizations in large corporations may have incentives that are not consistent with

groupware innovation. In this test, they could have been a big help but were instead a significant source of annoyance.

Groupware Used for Stage 4: Commitment/Decision Making

Task Sign-Ups at Team Meetings

At the weekly team meetings, team members "signed up" for specific tasks. The team leader managed this process, using one-on-one meetings as needed to encourage people either to sign up for new tasks or to follow through on ones to which they had already committed. Flip charts or the copyboard were often used to record who had committed to do what, sometimes with hard copy produced at the end of the meeting.

Electronic Messaging

The team leader used LINK to verify commitments and create a subtle form of peer pressure for team members to deliver on their commitments.

IBIS Methodology

By having a clear process, the IBIS consultants provided a framework for prioritizing work and structuring commitments. Team members knew what they were signing up to accomplish.

Stage 5: Implementation

For the TPP teams, the questions of "How will we do it?" and "Who does what, when, and where?" were resolved with relatively little effort. In fact, there was a strong voluntary mood on Team A— in spite of the fact that most of the team members also had other major responsibilities. This is an action-oriented company, and everyone wanted to get on with the work. The members of Team

A felt they were involved in an orchestrated effort where each person understood what she or he had to do and when. Each felt she or he was on track and almost always on schedule.

The implementation specifics were derived from the IBIS methodology but were adapted considerably to conform with the environment of Magnus Corporation. At weekly team meetings, tasks were identified on large time lines, with designations of what needed to be done and when—including who was responsible for getting tasks done. At each weekly team meeting, progress reports were made by each team member pursuing a task. Progress was charted on the time line, as well as on the task lists that were part of the methodology being used during the pilot.

Team A developed a way of implementing that began with what they came to call a "strawperson" version. This early draft of the implementation would then be critiqued, refined, and implemented—all in a tight circle of time. The team used this as a first step in implementation, to avoid biting off more than they could chew or to avoid making a major implementation mistake. The strawperson version was a low-risk way to get implementation going without risking the whole effort.

In addition, a specialized software package was acquired to help implement the specific procedures inherent in the methodology, but this package turned out to be of little value, largely because the adaptations that the team had to make made their needs different from the software's capabilities. Although software for common tasks did not prove useful to this team, simple and standardized (within their team) display formats did. For example, reporting formats were developed for interview results—springing from the methodology they were using during the pilot test. Some of these templates relied upon simple graphics, such as matrices or arrows. These straightforward templates proved very useful as a group tool, providing a standard framework within which data could be analyzed and results reported.

The scheduling and implementation for Team A went extremely well during the pilot. An aggressive schedule was held to without exception. The implementation process went extremely well indeed.

Lessons Learned Regarding Implementation

1. Sophisticated software for implementation of team tasks can be more difficult to use and less valuable than expected.

2. A leader skilled at electronic messaging can use it to keep the pace and keep the team current with breaking events.

3. Simple graphic methods for schedule timelines can have great value, particularly if they are reinforced by follow-ups via other media.

4. Implementation benefits from "hedges" (such as the strawperson approach developed by this team) that allow the implementation process to move forward quickly while minimizing the risks inherent in implementation.

5. Once at the implementation stage, *different-time* groupware is particularly useful—since the group is moving so fast that it can not meet in person to coordinate what goes on between team meetings.

Groupware Used for Stage 5: Implementation

Weekly Team Meetings

These sessions were used for progress reports and checkpointing. The team leader in Team A drove this process in a very supportive way that was received well by the team. The weekly team meetings also helped the team keep on schedule and this track record fueled itself. The team members learned they could crank out high-quality results on time and came to assume that this pace had to be maintained. The weekly team meetings provided a sort of "drum beat" reminder of what needed to be done. The team members also reported they looked forward to the weekly meetings.

Electronic Messaging

Some of the participants used LINK to coordinate the various tasks involved in implementation. Most of the messages sent, however, were from the leader. Thus it was more of a dissemination medium than a group discussion medium for this team.

Shared Filing Software

One of the strategic planning tasks during the pilot involved gathering data and interviewing in various parts of the corporation. A special software package was purchased so that common filing and report procedures could be used. One person used the system most of the time, and it did not prove very useful to the team. The idea of shared filing, however, seems to have some utility if there is a better match between the tasks to be performed and the software. In this case, the results were disappointing. It is also important to note that this is a very computer-sophisticated user group, with a healthy dose of skepticism. They do not seem like the type of group that would show naive faith in software.

Graphic Action Plans

Using large sheets of newsprint and Post-Its of different sizes, timelines were drawn at three points during the pilot. The timeline was broken into weeks. Tasks and milestones were written on Post-Its and moved around until a time could be agreed upon and committed to. Color- or graphics-coded Post-Its were used to indicate specific types of tasks, such as those covered in team meetings or those discussed with the management advisory board. The timelines were photocopied so that each team member had one, and they were reviewed periodically during team meetings. A facilitator did the timeline during the early stages, but this role was picked up by team members and did not require complicated graphics or artistic skills.

Shared Templates

Simple shared text or graphics formats prove surprisingly useful for team members to compare results from varied sources and present their findings to the outside world. Group-oriented forms management systems might build on such templates and provide great value to teams. The key is to develop templates that are meaningful and useful to the team.

Stage 6: High Performance

Team A did reach a high performance level during the pilot test. They experienced the "Wow!" stage that many teams never reach. At their peak, the team members were very much in synch, sensing each other's moves and needs and responding accordingly. This is the stage of team behavior that has been likened to a fast break in basketball: You have a general sense of what you will do in advance, but the specifics are governed by instinct. There was very little negative energy and great amounts of positive energy. They were a team with a mission, a team on the move. The information they were getting from their project efforts was important information. They knew they could all use what they were learning in many other ways.

Team One, on the other hand, reached a point of diminishing returns. They experienced resistance from business entities to sharing information, and they got mixed signals from their own bosses. Their leader was not able to keep the team focused and active.

A Team Performance Inventory was administered midway. This showed that Team One was indeed in trouble. Individual interviews corroborated the inventory, and all decided that they had achieved the goals of the pilot and would serve the project best by quitting and drawing lessons from their pilot process. (It is important to note here that "failure" may in fact still constitute a successful pilot. Lessons were learned and—because this was a limited pilot—the downside effects were minimal.)

Team A took the same Team Performance Inventory, and the results showed strong alignment and commitment. Team A members reported that they felt their team was able to accomplish more than they were capable of as individuals. In fact, they felt they were achieving greater results than they had anticipated during the pilot. They were flexible in responding to changes, and people did not need to be reminded about which jobs they were to be doing.

Humor was common at the weekly team meetings of Team A. Members frequently would volunteer for tasks. The leader rarely had to ask somebody to do something; he just had to say something needed to be done. The differences in language and professional orientation did keep the process mired in long discussions for clarity, so it never fully attained the intuitive, flow state communications some high performing teams achieve.

The off-site meetings were integral to fueling the morale of the team. The mood of casual dress and relaxed atmosphere in off-site meetings seemed an important tonic to the tension of the office and the pressures to meet a very demanding schedule for the pilot. When an additional full-time person was added to the team about two-thirds through the pilot, he came into a team that was rolling. Since he was received well by the team, all he needed to do was support what was already under way.

Lessons Learned Regarding High Performance

1. For this team of high-tech people, the low-tech forms of groupware did the most to sustain high performance levels, although their shared use of LINK was an important factor.

2. The chemistry that develops within a team as it moves into a high-performance stage can be fragile and unpredictable. Single individuals with unresolved commitment issues or a leader who cannot build a self-directed spirit on the team can quash the chance of a team experiencing high performance.

3. *Different-time* groupware seems critical at this stage, because team members are working together so well that they anticipate each other's moves and simply do not always have the time to get together in person.

Groupware Used for Stage 6: High Performance

Team Meetings

These were the regular source of new energy for the team members.

Off-Site Meetings

Periodically, the off-site meetings provided a sense of perspective on the pilot and a renewed sense of commitment.

Feedback on Performance

The inventories, interviews, and strategy sessions with consultants helped keep perspective and flexibility. LINK team messaging and daily communication contributed greatly to the integration Team A achieved.

Stage 7: Renewal

The renewal stage of team process is marked by time devoted to learning and transition. The Technology Planning Project was quite conscious about handling this stage. Team A felt that they periodically reviewed their goals and renewed their commitments to them. They handled the introduction of new members well (although this only occurred a couple of times). Nobody was bored, and burnout was not perceived as a problem in spite of the intensity of the pilot.

The phasing out of Team One was another example of conscious attention to transition. What Team One learned was important—especially the importance of chartering a group well and making sure that the leader is someone who has natural trust from the team. The learnings were documented, and the team disappeared.

But the best reflection of Team A's success in this stage came at their last off-site meeting. The mood at the start of the meeting was like that of a funeral. There was an awkwardness and a thickness in the air. When people finally did start talking, there was a bristling argumentative style that was quite uncharacteristic of earlier team meetings. What was happening here?

Several team members recognized that the team was probably going through a type of grieving. It had been performing at high performance levels, but the end of the pilot period was approaching. Individuals were not sure whether they would be involved in follow-up activity. The top management champion who helped the initial TPP had become excited about implementing a Total Quality approach (discussed elsewhere in this book) after a trip to Japan, and the IBIS model with its heavy analytical quality had not taken hold in the company at large. So the process was, in fact, ending and was not likely to go on in this same, exciting way.

Overt articulations of these feelings helped, but the team's action orientation left them frustrated. Their process had moved well beyond testing the IBIS method to having formulated clear recommendations for change in business strategy, design of systems, implementation processes, operations, and management. They wanted these to be heard.

At the final off-site meeting Team A charted its history and took stock of what it had learned. There was no question that they had learned a lot about the challenges of technology implementation and cross-functional integration. They had also learned a lot about strategic planning and now knew that aligning the business managers was a necessary prerequisite to designing the technology. The next phases would find them all redeployed in another process with other tools. Would Total Quality or some other set of techniques provide the sweeping mandate they had sought in the beginning? Would the positive aspects of the IBIS methodology stay alive and increase Magnus Corporation's capacity to plan? Finally, the teams learned that team performance is a process, and the tools that helped were ones they could carry flexibly with them as they navigated through the ups and downs of Magnus Corporation's dynamic business.

Lessons Learned Regarding Renewal

1. An ending—even for a successful team—can be very painful, like a funeral.
2. Face-to-face meetings, particularly off-site ones, seem most appropriate for renewal activities, even for technical people.
3. Renewal and learning go hand in hand. It happens in a recurring way, even during an ad hoc pilot test period. When learning is a strong orientation, there are truly no failures, as each ending is a clear source of insight for new beginnings.

Groupware Used for Stage 7: Renewal

Off-Site Meetings

The off-site meetings had a definite renewal focus during this pilot, although this was typically not their stated goal.

Summary Reports

The team used writing to coalesce what they had learned and to frame new questions.

LINK Conference

A special conference on LINK, which involved many people from other parts of the organization, provided an ongoing forum for big questions and new insights.

Part V

Future Groupware Applications

24

Cross-Cultural Groupware

Cross-cultural groupware isn't exotic. It's more of the same problems that exist in organizations already and *lots* of the unexpected.

If your organization has difficulty with incompatible technology, imagine part of your group working in some place like Botswana, where there isn't much technology to speak of at all! And if you're unable to reach consensus in *same-time/same-place* meetings, try spreading it out over 18 time zones and two different calendar days (the distance between Tokyo and New York). Such a situation could mean instant chaos for content-oriented folks working in a mechanical model of an organization, in which all the pieces are known and programmable.

Working cross-culturally is a real test of an organization's process orientation. Even though it tends to be more detailed and

more complex, the process of developing and using tools for cross-cultural or global use is the same as working domestically. If groupware lets groups see themselves in a mirror, cross-cultural groupware is like watching time-lapse photography in that mirror, looking for patterns of motion.

Cross-cultural work may seem like a hot topic in U.S. business, but it's nothing new. Other cultures and countries have been dealing with our culture for scores of years, and some have it down—seamlessly. Now we have a good chance to learn from these other cultures and bring some of our creativity to the process. It even may be an opportunity to address hitherto hidden cultural issues within our own domestic business culture.

Two Projects, Four Continents

During this past year, while our team worked with prospective groupware users, some of our members also were completing two different international process design and collaborative publishing projects, headed for use in Kenya, Costa Rica, and Japan. We were in a lab on two continents and three islands, working with team members who spoke English (U.S. and British), Spanish, and Japanese, and spanning some 15 time zones and the international date line. Luckily for us, our publishing projects weren't all in the same stage at the same time!

One project involved the collaborative development of instructional materials for nursing instructors and used our raw experience in "collaborative publishing" as a model to empower instructors all over the world to do the same. Our hope is that the process will replicate itself as needed in widening circles. So modeling the process ourselves meant riding the wave of an unfolding adventure without much precedent to follow. It also made us pretty self-conscious.

The glue here is love and a good sense of humor. Our meetings are filled with admiration for each other's fields, stories about "the most amazing food I was ever served" on a trip, and commitment to the ultimate goal (as put forth by the United Nations) "Health for All by the Year 2000." We also send funny drawings back and forth on faxes to relieve the grayness of thermafax paper.

Graphic language is another sort of team glue. We use it to flesh out the training materials at our big-group face-to-face meetings (about twice a year). We create wall-sized group memories of team meetings, and we use this method in all instructor workshops to help visualize processes and goals. Sometimes the poster paper rolls travel with fishing rods in a tube, sometimes there is no poster paper at all, and the classified newspaper ads serve as a grid for a matrix diagram.

As we talk and draw about ourselves we often use the Team Performance Model as a guide for design and teaching. It has been adapted in many ways to display instructional processes. Yet there were surprises, too. One major instructional project for nurses in Costa Rica was designed around team building and the Team Performance model—until the facilitator realized that the team concept was utterly foreign to nurses there.

In the United States, we usually keep in touch by phone, but because of budget constraints international communication is mostly via fax. If we had read the literature on groupware use before launching into things we would have developed a set of fax templates earlier, to help wade through all the information we sloshed back and forth. As it happened, team members walked in to their office one day to find a partly handwritten, partly "refaxed" 32-page document on the floor!

Since we weren't connected by computer modem, our electronic information had to go on diskettes by mail or international courier. What a shock it was to find out that the courier company didn't consider diskettes "documents," but dutiable items!

Since we're all glued to our personal computers, they became a standard feature in these two projects, even though one team member had to hand carry her machine on the plane to Costa Rica and then share it with three other people. We discovered that personal computers can't do with Japanese what they can do with English, and that the technology isn't yet versatile enough in Japan.

Our cultural "translators" became a groupware tool, because they could regularly inform us and help reshape the way we worked. One told us that the graphics of little androgynous figures were too hard for nurses, who work so closely and constantly with children and adults, to identify with. They had to have eyes. Another translator told us that we couldn't use our growth metaphor and draw models underground—it brought up too many images of employment and social oppression. We learned about the translation of things between other cultures, too: nutrition in Central America versus nutrition in Africa.

What the translators brought back affected us deeply and made us think about those once faceless figures, and more.

Suggestions About Methods

"Back to Basics": Pay Attention to the Obvious and Essential

- Take the time to be scrupulously clear about all roles and responsibilities, especially as they relate to the first three stages of the Team Performance Model.
- Establish mutually agreed upon ground rules for procedures and communications, and review them from time to time. What will the ramifications be if procedures aren't followed? Have back-up plans for everything.
- Find out what your team "glue" is—what holds it together—and propagate it.
- Have at least one person at each location who can "speak" each of the other distinct cultures, to act as a translator. Check out plans with translators before undertaking big projects in unfamiliar surroundings.

"If It's Lunchtime Here, You Must Be Asleep": Consider Time

- Be aware of other team members' working hours (so they don't have to be "cyber" and take calls at 3:00 A.M.).
- Leave extra time for everything, especially Customs "Services," national holidays, last minute redesign of materials, and the self-reflection brought about by this process.
- Try to break the time barrier occasionally and plan for a few *same-time/same-place* meetings to renew team spirit and celebrate your survival.

"Tee Up Those Sacred Cows": *Be Prepared to Change*

- Expect incompatible (or totally unavailable) technology, and be prepared to settle for something inelegant but practical (a workbook layout simple enough to be typed and mimeographed on-site, for example).

- Always expect the unimaginable and even be prepared to redesign the project, if that's what's called for.

- Listen to the team members who act as cultural and language translators, and let that knowledge change you personally. And, while you're at it, make an attempt to get out of your first language—even for the exercise.

If nothing else, just keeping expectations to a manageable level can be a big help. After all, it's a global trek we're on—not a foot race.

25

Groupware in Grade Schools

Educational technologies span a range of student/teacher interaction and the variety of teaching methods they support. A computer-based "smart tutor" can put the student through drill/workbook exercises at the student's own pace. At the other end of the spectrum, electronic-mail-based projects (using a computer and modem) that link several classrooms and encourage cooperative work seem to offer the most opportunities for teamwork. Although educational technology is not directly responsible for creating teamwork in the classroom, as a tool it can allow the teacher to work with a more cooperative teaching style.

The following scenario describes the evolution of a cooperative learning environment that could potentially exist when telecommunications links classrooms in educational projects. This scenario is based on real experiences during this last year of the Groupware Users' Project.

Classrooms Connect On-line

The 12:15 lunch bell rang, but Franklin Middle School's sixth grade history class lingered in the classroom. A group of students huddled in one corner pushing pins into a wall-sized world map, marking the four electronic class-rooms that comprised their on-line project cluster for the new semester: one in a small rural town in Northern California, another in upstate New York, a third classroom in Israel, and the final classroom which seemed to the kids to be in a place almost off the map—Australia. All the classes were middle school history and geography classes planning to study and learn cooperatively using an educational networking service.

In the previous week, the Franklin sixth graders and their teacher, Mrs. Barnes, brainstormed project topics to study and sent a list of ideas to the other classrooms via a shared mailbox on the network. The four teachers settled on two project themes to frame their writing exchanges and research—discovering and exchanging local legends, and researching and documenting the local history and geography of each class' community. The group leader—Moske Eber, the teacher from Israel—reviewed the curriculum objectives with each teacher, then listed tasks for the project, including interviewing family and community leaders, creating a database with local legends and geographical discoveries, and final production of a magazine/publication that compiled the writings and visuals collected throughout the semester.

Global Magazine. The class was excited to work with other students in different states and countries through the network. But more importantly, as they began interviewing their grandparents about their town's origins to share over the network, the students realized they were creating historical accounts—and writing history. They realized their writing had to be clear and imaginative to convey their town's history to their group partners.

By the eighth week of the semester, the day-to-day operations of Mrs. Barnes' class had nearly been transformed. Before each task group reported to the whole class on their activities, one student read new messages from the network and gave copies to the relevant task groups. The role of mail distributor changed every two weeks so that all the students would become familiar with accessing E-mail via the computer and modem. A local Tasmanian legend came in from their friends in Australia about drought, and a response came to a survey on local slang; the classes in Israel and Northern California sent their accounts of how their local governments operate.

Some Ground Rules Emerge. At the project's start the classes agreed on network etiquette that would help them perform their tasks on time and keep group participation regular. Some ground rules were (1) mail would be signed and checked at least once a week; (2) outgoing mail would always be sent at the end of the week; (3) if a class could not meet a deadline in response to a survey or exchange of material, a message would be sent stating so. The ground rules also were intended to quell the frustration of not knowing whether cluster members were on-line or were having technical problems, and were a courtesy to the other cluster members to keep in touch.

When the semester was almost over, the students had generated a lot of information—legends, answers to surveys, and historical accounts. The goal for the semester was to have a finished publication that each class could circulate to other classes in their own school, put in the library, and share with teachers and friends who helped along the way.

Mrs. Barnes' class presented to the principal a copy of the final report and explained how they had accomplished it over an electronic network. Mrs. Barnes explained, "The impact on the class's learning is perhaps the greatest outcome. The kids had a real need and reason to undertake their tasks. The project put them in the concrete area of learning rather than exclusively in the abstract. The students saw the need to write, to plan, and to prepare a project; and they gained a better understanding of the role of computers within the learning curriculum."

Students commented, "[this project] keeps me in touch with local and national events and domestic and foreign problems. I see how people in foreign countries and in America live compared to my own little community," and "Doing this project tied many of my subjects together, and they made sense. I learned history and writing, how to research a problem, and how to ask questions."

Interaction and Cooperative Learning

Several educational services are emerging—some commercial and some still in the trial stage—that provide electronic mail bulletin board systems for grades K through 12. They range from loosely organized E-mail exchanges to highly structured messaging based on curriculum objectives (which appear to have more educational value). The idea behind them is that while different classrooms across the country are working together on a local history project, for example, each class must assume certain responsibilities for the completion of the group project.

Within the classroom, students break up into teams that perform different tasks: research, interviews, compiling data/ text, exchanging mail, etc., that require coordination. The tasks usually rotate so that students learn many skills. Students and teachers evaluate responses from other classes working on their project who are likely to be in a different geographical location, thus adding a cultural dimension to the exchanges. Interactive E-mail enables cooperative learning and teaching with groups that are not face to face and can enhance the need for good communication, organization skills, and teamwork among students and teachers.

Some teachers have said that in years of teaching they have not seen kids as excited about learning and writing effectively as they are with networking class projects. Others have remarked that their students now ask to work in groups rather than individually to solve problems and complete projects.

More specifically, such a learning environment encourages many workplace skills, such as the abilities to follow schedules and deadlines and to use creative group processes like brainstorming. Kids learning in this kind of environment will most likely be better equipped than their predecessors to assimilate well into the future workforce. Increasingly, the workplace is broken down into project teams, task forces, and goal-oriented workgroups. The need for clear and effective communication and analytical thinking has never been more important.

In his study *Technology and the Transformation of Schools*,[1] Louis Perelman, a leader in educational and technological innovation, says that today's classrooms, with teachers as the main source of information and students as passive receivers of information, will not produce the kind of youth to carry the United States into the future. Perelman and other education advocates remark that curricula need to be redesigned so they encourage students to become problem solvers and decision makers. Perelman specifically notes that students must be able to "generate new knowledge and control situations." Without skills for the information economy, the gap between school and work widens, and the alignment of America's youth with the future economy and society will be lost.

What are the unique attributes of educational technology that will help education evolve into a new kind of learning environment for the future? The strengths of telecommunications-based services are their capacity to access and exchange information quickly across large distances. These attributes can encourage teachers to develop curriculum projects that create a meaningful environment that transcends the classroom. Reading, writing, critical thinking, and research skills thus become valued tools. In addition, an electronic network connects otherwise isolated students with their peers, bringing our increasingly global society into individual classrooms; and such a network offers students new perspectives and understanding of the world.

There are, however, two important caveats that constrain educational technology. School budgets and sources of funding are highly uncertain from year to year and are often allocated to basic and essential purchases in school districts. Educational technology easily can get scratched from the budget when funds are tight. Another limitation particular to telecommunications services is that schools find it quite difficult to access individual, dedicated phone lines. Most school phone systems operate through a central switchboard, which presents difficulties in trying to connect via a modem when lines are busy.

The groupware concept, as it exists in some telecommunications-based networking services for schools, seems to be close to being a tool that could empower classrooms to transform themselves into the "classroom of the future." As one educational networker, Dr. Margaret Riel, says, "The starting point is not technology, but the educational goals that can be accomplished by the use of technology." Groupware tools, networking tools, and the like may help teachers realize their goals of reform and restructuring in the classroom—the way those very tools have helped business teams reach goals, manage crises, and carry their work into the next decade.

References

1. L.J. Perelman. *Technology and the Transformation of Schools.* Alexandria, Va.: ITTE Technology Leadership Network, 1987.

Part VI

Epilogue

26

Groupware Comes of Age

Groupware is here to stay—whatever it comes to be called. Business teams and flexible organizational forms will drive the need for groupware—the tools that help groups work collaboratively. And as teamwork strategies gain appeal, the need for improvements on costly and often inefficient face-to-face meetings will only increase. The only uncertainties about groupware are just how its emergence will occur, how long it will take, and who will make money from the process.

In this epilogue, we look beyond the Groupware Users' Project to speculate about future directions. What approaches to groupware use are likely to yield the biggest payoffs in the near future? What steps can be taken now to increase the probability of desirable futures and to decrease the probability of undesirable ones? As a starting point for answering these future-oriented questions, we have taken stock of what has been learned about groupware thus far.

Look again at the hybrid of the 4-Square Map and the Team Performance Model, shown in Fig. 26.1. Now think of this model as a back-of-the-envelope sketch of groupware in the future. In the abstract, it's a first approximation of how electronic and nonelectronic groupware tools might be applied to the varied needs of business teams. But it is important to bring some life to this abstract model and extend it into the future—so we have

Figure 26.1
Preferred Groupware Options for Team Performance

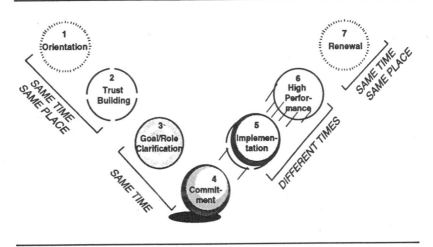

created a set of brief scenarios about groupware approaches between now and 1995.

In creating these scenarios, we used the hybrid model as a beginning checklist and stimulus. We have also drawn from conversations with other organizations that are pilot testing groupware, as well as the work of other researchers. If these dawning days of the information age are at all parallel to the age of exploration back in the 15th century, then these scenarios are the first, best composites of the maps, routes of passage, and types of teams that will ply these new opportunities. Main features will remain. Details will fill out as organizations actually make use of the new tools.

The following scenarios provide a taste of the groupware user approaches we think will be yielding the most value by 1995 (though actual use may not necessarily be widespread). We have made the scenarios brief because they are intended to be more provocative than comprehensive. We wanted to summarize our thoughts, but also to provoke your thoughts. We have put them in what we feel is an approximate order of difficulty, although we feel that all of them are believable within the next five years.

Groupware 1995

High-Tech/High-Touch Groupware

As organizations have become increasingly "infomated" (Shoshanna Zuboff's word[1]) with more data than can possibly be absorbed by individuals, special high-tech/high-touch rooms have emerged that make use of group intelligence, augmented by feeds from the outside world, special group memory processors, and information refineries that let the group track and organize large quantities of information. This conceptual intensity is balanced with flexible break-out capabilities for specialized activities including exercise, variable work arrangements, and even play. Institutional memories are searchable and retrievable to provide rich contextual information to all parts of an organization's decision-making areas.

Electronic networks have made organizational "sensing" more than a metaphor. Over time, the historical bias of such databases has been balanced by visionary "agents" provided by key managers and the strategic planning process of the organization itself. Virtual teams are formed to champion specific ideas and keep them alive in the memory. Bubble-ups and meltdowns, of course, require reconstructions and maintenance.

High-tech/high-touch rooms are scattered about large organizations; managers are trained in their use, and special facilitators are used for complex meetings. These *same-time/ same-place* computer-assisted meeting rooms are now practical for large businesses in 1990, with rapid growth beginning in 1993.

Conflict-Resolution Centers

Conflict-resolution techniques have been combined with electronic groupware to create special centers geared toward resolving controversies. In these *same-time/same-place* centers (specialized versions of the high-tech/high-touch rooms discussed above), software tools such as stakeholder analysis and anonymous voting allow people with strong differences to work together. Team leaders and meeting facilitators use the various electronic tools judiciously; there are no mechanical resolutions to many controversies.

Cross-Cultural Groupware

As international business and exchange has become more commonplace, there are more and more situations where people must communicate with others via what is, for them, a second or third language. *Same-time/same-place* groupware (another variation on the high-tech/high-touch rooms described above) allows participants to see written versions of what is being discussed—providing a more equal footing for cross-language communications. Also, special computer-aided translation augments both real-time and store-and-forward meetings. Meeting facilitators are an important part of many of these exchanges.

Workflow Structuring

Building on the base of electronic mail and voice mail, a variety of structures, or "forms," have emerged to speed the conduct of intracompany and even intercompany exchanges. After deciding that early attempts at conversational structuring in the late 1980s were too heavy-handed, a splash of new products appeared in the early 1990s to provide various structural overlays for communications via electronic mail and voice mail. Also, organizations have designed their own formats and interfaces, depending on cultural and other needs of their businesses. The use of common forms and templates allows for rapid communications and also practical forms of message filtering, thus greatly reducing quantities of electronic junk mail.

TQ Groupware

As discussed earlier in this book, Total Quality (TQ) was introduced to many U.S. businesses in the late 1980s. By now, in 1995, TQ is a way of life for the majority of the *Fortune* 500, with accompanying needs for business teams and tools to support TQ techniques. These tools function in all four quadrants of the 4-Square Map of Groupware Options, but the emphasis is on *same time/same place.*

Market-Research Groupware

Building on the infrastructure of market-research centers in major U.S. cities (for the conduct of focus groups and other forms of market research), special *same-time/same-place* rooms have been built. In these rooms, special software allows for questionnaire techniques such as conjoint (paired choice comparisons) and Likert scales (multiple choice options on numeric scales), with instant analysis and feedback to participants. Some of these tools are also adapted for *same-time/different-place* market research with audio or video links. The latter tools are used most commonly for market research among specialized segments that are typically hard to reach, such as medical doctors.

Orientation Simulators

Building on the model of aircraft simulators for training pilots, this form of groupware uses simulation to introduce people to new organizations or environments. For example, one type of orientation simulator is designed for new hires in large companies. These systems can be used by a group, *same-time/same-place,* or individually, *different-times/different-places.*

Graphic hypertext databases allow trainers to create high-dimension simulation environments to orient new employees to the history, projects, capabilities, and strategies of their employers.

Virtual "Skunkworks"

Geographically separated teams have been working together using *different-time/different-place* groupware to coordinate global projects and operations. Like the original 1950s skunkworks at Northrop Corporation, these teams have been operating with a minimum of management bureaucracy and control. These "invisible colleges" have their own disciplines for working together at a distance and accomplishing massive tasks. They have tasks like global opportunity scanning, sales, market trading, or information gathering. Some of these groups are ongoing professional exchanges in areas where expertise is important, but where day-to-day assignments are out with line business areas, rather than in cloistered specialty groups. Thus, the energy and productivity of a skunkworks operation is maintained at a distance via groupware.

Crisis Response Teams

These are world-class teams that handle crises such as oil spill clean-ups, toxic emergencies, or other disasters that demand quick action. Crisis response teams compress time in any way that they can, making heavy use of electronic groupware. Their whole experience is in fast forward, with groupware capable of adjusting to the rapid shifts. The team members are like other emergency personnel: bored 95% of the time while training and waiting, but highly energized the 5% of the time they are actually working. Crisis response teams use *same time / same place* and *same time / different place*. The *same-time* orientation is critical during a crisis. They also have a *same-place / different-time* team room they use as home base. High-dimension simulators are essential "workout equipment" at these bases.

Teleconference Groupware

Building on the existing installed base of video teleconference rooms (finally, the installed base of two-way video rooms in North America has grown to more than 1000) and the increasing use of conference calls, a new market for groupware in teleconference rooms and systems appeared. Slowly at first, then with increasing speed, these tools were added onto the installed base. In some cases, teleconferencing was added to *same-time / same-place* groupware rooms to provide similar capabilities.

Groupware Presentation Builders

As people rediscovered that the medium is, after all, at least a message, teams began to use video, software, print, workshop, and presentation design tools as groupware to draw out, focus, package, and communicate their ideas to larger audiences. Working directly in these different media has become increasingly possible through groupware advances. Also, media production has become more accessible to nonartistic teams, and professional production people have become more collaborative.

Dyna-Meetings

Dynabooks (Alan Kay's original vision of an ultralight computer—his criterion was that you should be able to carry your dynabook and two bags of groceries at the same time) have become so widespread that they have formed a new infrastructure on which groupware has been built. This special groupware facilitates dyna-meetings, a kind of pluggable networking available in the regular business hotels and better restaurants. "Check available times" functions or "flag shared resources" functions will allow teams to "infomate" at will. Dyna-meetings allow true *any-time / any-place* groupware, finally. . . .

Final Words

Groupware as we know it today is little more than a peek at a new world. Our conclusion from the Groupware Users' Project is that the impact of groupware will be very big. It is not just another new class of software products. In fact, it may not be a product class at all, but a name pointing to a structural shift in the very perspective of tool designers and of organizations. The key structural shift is from thinking of users as individuals to thinking of them as collaborative teams.

At one time, it was possible to believe (wishfully) that information technology alone would advance humanity. But as electronic tools have insinuated themselves into every part of our business and private lives, we now demand that technology take into account the whole human being, including the social and relational aspects of life. Groupware focuses on these social and relational aspects; the technology is clearly secondary.

Groupware is a probe into a very important new zone: the team-driven, flexible organization of the future. Our work documented in this book has shown that groupware can deliver immediate results for teams that are willing to pursue simultaneously both electronic and nonelectronic approaches. Such leading business teams are on the frontier; they are roughing in the organization of the 1990s. Groupware will be critical to the performance of teams in the near future, and teams will be critical to the future of organizations. The process of leading business teams will increasingly require an ability to make intelligent use of both electronic and nonelectronic groupware tools.

References

1. Zuboff, S. *In the Age of the Smart Machine: The Future of Work and Power.* New York: Basic Books, 1988.

Bibliography

Bair, J. H. "The need for collaboration tools in offices." *Office Automation Conference 1985 Digest* (Feb. 4–6):1985.

Bennis, W. *Why Leaders Can't Lead: The Unconscious Conspiracy Continues.* San Francisco, Calif.: Jossey-Bass, 1989.

Blackler, F., and C. Brown. "Evaluation and the impact of information technologies on people in organizations." *Human Relations* 38(Mar. 1985)3:213–231.

Blake, R. R., and J. S. Mouton. *The New Managerial Grid.* Houston, Tex.: Gulf, 1978.

Bowen, W. "The puny payoff from office computers." *Fortune Magazine* (May 26, 1986):20–24.

Bradford, L. P., J. R. Gibb, and K. D. Benne. *T-Group Theory and Laboratory Method: Innovation in Re-Education.* J. Wiley, 1967.

Bullen, C. V., and J. L. Bennett. *Groupware in Practice: An Interpretation of Work Experience.* Cambridge, Mass.: MIT, Center for Information Systems Research, 1990.

Burke, W. W. *Organization Development: Principles and Practice.* Boston, Mass.: Little Brown, 1982.

Cash, J. I., Jr., and P. L. McLeod. "Managing the introduction of information systems technology in strategically dependent companies." *Journal of Management Information Systems* 1(Spring 1985)4:5–22.

"Catch the team spirit: The great experiment in team management." *Across the Board* 26(May 1989):5.

Cespedes, F. V., S. X. Doyle, and R. J. Freedman. "Teamwork for today's selling." *Harvard Business Review* (Mar.–Apr. 1989):44-58.

Charles, J. "Approaches to teleconferencing justification: Towards a general model." *Telecommunications Policy* 12(1981):296–303.

Crosby, P. B. *Quality Is Free: The Art of Making Quality Certain.* New York: Mentor Books, 1979.

Cullen, J., and J. Hollingum. *Implementing Total Quality.* Bedford, U.K.: IFS Publications, Ltd., 1987.

Davis, S. M. *Future Perfect.* Reading, Mass.: Addison-Wesley, 1987.

DeMarco, T., and T. Lister. *Peopleware: Productive Projects and Teams.* New York: Dorset House, 1987.

Deming, W. E. *Out of the Crisis.* Cambridge, Mass.: Center for Advanced Engineering Study, 1988.

Dennis, A. R., J. F. George, L. M. Jessup, J. F. Nunamaker, Jr., and D. R. Vogel. "Information technology to support electronic meetings." *MIS Quarterly* 12(Dec. 1988)4:591–624.

DeSancitis, G., and B. Gallupe. "A foundation for the study of group decision support systems." *Management Science* 33(May 1987):5.

DeSanctis, G., M. Poole, M. Limayem, and W. Johnson. *The GDSS Research Project: Experimental Materials Summary and General Questionnaires.* Minneapolis, Minn.: Management Information Systems Research Center, April 1990.

Doyle, M., and D. Straus. *The Interaction Method: How to Make Meetings Work.* New York: Jove Books, 1976.

Drexler, A. B., D. Sibbet, and R. H. Forrester. "The team performance model." *Team Building: Blueprints for Productivity.* W. B. Reddy and K. Jamison (eds.). San Diego, Calif.: National Training Laboratory, Institute for Behavioral Sciences, 1988:45–61.

Drucker, P. F. The coming of the new organization." *Harvard Business Review.* (Jan.–Feb. 1988):45–53.

Drucker, P. F. *The New Realities.* New York: Harper and Row, 1989.

Dyer, W. G. *Team Building: Issues and Alternatives.* Reading, Mass.: Addison-Wesley, 1987.

Ellis, C. A., S. J. Gibbs, and G. L. Rein. *Groupware: The Research and Development Issues.* Austin, Tex.: Microelectronics and Computer Technology Corporation, 1988.

Flores, F., M. Graves, B. Hartfield, and T. Winograd. "Computer systems and the design of organizational interaction." *ACM Transactions on Office Information Systems* 6(April 1988)2:153–172.

Galbraith, J. R. *Designing Complex Organizations*. Reading, Mass.: Addison-Wesley, 1973.

Galbraith, J. R., and D. A. Nathanson. *Strategy Implementation: The Role of Structure and Process*. St. Paul, Minn.: West, 1978.

Gibb, J. R. *Trust: A New View of Personal and Organizational Development*. Los Angeles, Calif.: Guild of Tutors Press, 1978.

Gleick, J. *Chaos: Making a New Science*. New York: Viking Penguin, 1987.

Gray, B. *Collaborating: Finding Common Ground for Multiparty Problems*. San Francisco, Calif.: Jossey-Bass, 1989.

Gray, P. *Decision Support Systems*. North-Holland: Elsevier Science, 1987.

Gray, P., D. Vogel, and R. Beauclair. "Assessing GDSS empirical research." *European Journal of Operations Research* (Spring 1990).

Greif, I. (ed.). *Computer-Supported Cooperative Work: A Book of Readings*. San Mateo, Calif.: Morgan Kaufmann, 1988.

Hanna, D. P. *Designing Organizations for High Performance*. Reading, Mass.: Addison-Wesley, 1988.

Hauser, J. R., and D. Clausing. "The house of quality." *Harvard Business Review* (May–June 1988):63–73.

Hersey, P., and K. H. Blanchard. *Management of Organizational Behavior* (1st edition). Englewood Cliffs, N.J.: Prentice-Hall, 1969.

Hoerr, J. "The payoff from teamwork." *Business Week* (July 10, 1989):56.

Huber, G. P. "Issues in the design of group decision support systems." *MIS Quarterly* (Sept. 1984):195–204.

Johansen, R. *Groupware: Computer Support for Business Teams*. New York: The Free Press, 1988.

Juran, J. M. (ed.). *Quality Control Handbook*. New York: McGraw-Hill, 1974.

Keen, P. G. W. *Competing in Time*. Cambridge, Mass.: Ballinger, 1986.

Kotter, J. P. *The Leadership Factor.* New York: The Free Press, 1988.

Kraemer, K., and J. King. "Computer-based systems for cooperative work." *Computing Surveys* 20(June, 1988)2:115–146.

Kraut, R. E. (ed.). *Technology and the Transformation of White-Collar Work.* Hillsdale, N.J.: Lawrence Elbaum Associates, 1987.

Lai, K. Y., T. W. Malone, and K. C. Yu. "Object Lens: A 'spreadsheet' for cooperative work." *ACM Transaction on Office Information Systems* (Oct. 1988).

Larson, C. E., and F. M. J. LaFasto. *Teamwork: What Must Go Right, What Can Go Wrong.* Newbury Park, Calif.: Sage Publications, 1989.

Malone, T. W. *What Is Coordination Theory?* Cambridge, Mass.: Massachusetts Institute of Technology. Paper presented at the National Science Foundation Coordination Theory Workshop, February 19, 1988.

Malone, T. W., K. R. Grant, F. A. Turbak, S. A. Brobst, and M. D. Cohen. "Intelligent information-sharing systems." *Communications of the ACM* 30(1987)5:390–402.

Malone, T. W., K. R. Grant, K. Y. Lai, R. Rao, and D. A. Rosenblitt. "Semistructured messages are surprisingly useful for computer-supported coordination." *ACM Transaction on Office Information Systems* 5(1987)2:115–131.

—— "The information lens: An intelligent system for information sharing and coordination." In *Technological Support for Work Group Collaboration.* M. H. Olsen (ed.). Hillsdale, N.J.: Erlbaum, 1989.

Martin, A. *Focus on Group Processes, Not Just Technology.* Torrance, Calif.: I/S Analyzer (July 1989).

Maslow, A. H. *Toward a Psychology of Being.* Princeton, N.J.: Van Nostrand, 1962.

Merrills, R. "How Northern Telecom competes on time." *Harvard Business Review* (July–Aug. 1989):108–144.

Meyer, N. D., and M. E. Boone. *The Information Edge.* New York: McGraw-Hill, 1987.

Mosvick, R. K., and R. B. Nelson. *We've Got to Start Meeting Like This.* Glenview, Ill.: Scott, Foresman Professional Publishing Group, 1987.

Myers, I. B. *The Myers-Briggs Type Indicator.* Palo Alto, Calif.: Consulting Psychologists Press, 1962.

Nunamaker, J. F., L. M. Applegate, and B. R. Konsynski. "Computer-aided deliberation: Model management and group decision support." *Operations Research* 36(Nov.–Dec., 1988)6:826–848.

Nunamaker, J. F., D. Vogel, A. Heminger, B. Martz, R. Grohowski, and C. McGoff. "Experiences at IBM with group support systems: A field study." *Decision Support Systems* 5(1989):183–196.

Olson, M. H. *Technological Support for Work Group Collaboration.* Hillsdale, N.J.: Lawrence Erlbaum Associates, 1989.

Ost, E. J. "Team-based pay: New wave strategic incentives." *Sloan Management Review* (Spring 1990):19–27.

Perelman, L. J. *Technology and the Transformation of Schools.* Alexandria, Va.: ITTE Technology Leadership Network, 1987.

Pinsonneault, A., and K. L. Kraemer. "The impact of technological support on groups: An assessment of the empirical research." *Decision Support Systems* 5(1989):197–216.

Piore, M. J., and C. F. Sabel. *The Second Industrial Divide: Possibilities for Prosperity.* New York: Basic Books, 1984.

Reddy, B. W., and K. Jamison, (eds.). *Team-Building: Blueprints for Productivity and Satisfaction.* San Diego, Calif.: University Associates, 1988.

Reich, R. B. "Entrepreneurship reconsidered: The team as hero." *Harvard Business Review* (May–June 1987):77–83.

Richman, L. S. "Software catches the team spirit." *Fortune* (June 8, 1987):125–133.

Rockart, J. F., and C. V. Bullen. *The Rise of Managerial Computing.* Homewood, Ill.: Dow Jones-Irwin, 1986.

Rockart, J. F., and D. W. DeLong. *Executive Support Systems.* Homewood, Ill.: Dow Jones Irwin, 1988.

Rogers, E. M. *Communication Technology: The New Media in Society.* New York: The Free Press, 1986.

Schutz, W. *FIRO: A Three-Dimensional Theory of Interpersonal Behavior.* Muir Beach, Calif.: WSA, 1989. Original publication 1959.

Sibbet, D. *I See What You Mean: A Workbook Guide to Group Graphics.* San Francisco, Calif.: Graphic Guides, 1980 (to be republished in 1991).

Sikes, W. W., A. Drexler, and J. Gant. *The Emerging Practice of Organizational Development*. NTL Institute for Applied Behavioral Science and University Associates, 1989.

Stefik, M. "The next knowledge medium." *The AI Magazine* (Spring 1986):34–46.

Tubbs, S. L. *A Systems Approach to Small Group Interaction*. Reading, Mass.: Addison-Wesley, 1984.

Tuckman, B. W. "Developmental sequence in small groups." *Psychological Bulletin* 63(1965):384–399.

Vaill, P. B. *Managing as a Performing Art*. San Francisco, Calif.: Jossey-Bass, 1989.

Vogel, D. R., J. F. Nunamaker, J. F. George, and A. R. Dennis. "Group decision support systems: Evolution and status at the University of Arizona." In *Organizational Decision Support Systems*. North-Holland: Elsevier Science Publishers B.V., 1988.

Vogel, D., J. Nunamaker, B. Martz, R. Grohowski, and C. McGoff. "Electronic meeting system experience at IBM." *Journal of MIS* (1989).

Waterman, R. H., Jr. *Adhocracy: The Power to Change*. Knoxville, Tenn.: Whittle Direct Books, 1990.

Weisbord, M.R. *Productive Workplaces: Organizing and Managing for Dignity, Meaning, and Community*. San Francisco, Calif.: Jossey-Bass, 1987.

———. Organizational Diagnosis. Reading, Mass.: Addison-Wesley, 1978 (1985 printing).

Young, A. M. *The Reflexive Universe: Evolution of Consciousness*. New York: Delacorte Press/S. Lawrence, 1976.

Zuboff, S. *In the Age of the Smart Machine: The Future of Work and Power*. New York: Basic Books, 1988.